A PICTORIAL TREASURY OF

IN AMERICA

By DANIEL BLUM

NEW YORK

GROSSET & DUNLAP

Publishers

Acknowledgements

I wish to thank the following for the loan of pictures and assistance in compiling this book: T. M. Salisbury, Charles Nolte, John Willis, May Davenport Seymour, Walter Latwaite, the late Vernon Rice, William H. Seltsam, Maynard Morris, Theodore M. Purdy, Jean Gillette, Francis Robinson, Mrs. John DeWitt Peltz, William H. Matthews, George Freedley, Earle Forbes, J. Charles Gilbert, Brandt Aymar, and all the opera stars whose cooperation was so helpful. Also, the Metropolitan Opera Guild, the Metropolitan Opera House Library, the New York City Opera Company, the San Francisco Opera Company, the New York Public Library, the Museum of The City of New York, the New York Post and Culver Service.

ALSO

Louis Melancon and Sedge Le Blang whose photographs of the more recent Metropolitan Opera Company productions and stars enhance this book.

TO

MY SISTER DOROTHY

—whose love and understanding

have brought great happiness into my life

Early Years
of Opera
in America

The political and religious refugees who colonized North America in the seventeenth century limited their artistic expression to religious songs and services, and it was not until the growth of the cities of the eastern seaboard that the first theatres made their appearance. Grand opera, reflecting the splendor and divinity of absolute monarchy and the ritual and sumptuousness of the Catholic Church, had no place in the hard world of the new continent. It is understandable that early attempts at opera were patterned after *The Beggar's Opera* and other such ballad pieces. Charleston, South Carolina, witnessed the first recorded performance of opera in America, a production of *Flora,* or *Hob in the Well,* given on the 18th of February, 1735. The opera was an import from England and became an American favorite for many years. During the next fifty years this and other early ballad operas were performed frequently in the new cities of Baltimore, Williamsburg,

**Jenny Lind as
"The Daughter of The Regiment"**

Pauline Lucca

Philadelphia, New York, and Boston. Early New Yorkers used to travel uptown to the Nassau Street Theatre for their opera, and already performances were occasions for social display. At the time of the Revolution opera was given at the John Street Theatre, and on one occasion the new President Washington sat in a box to hear *The Temple of Minerva,* an oratorio opera, which was composed by Francis Hopkinson, one of the signers of the Declaration of Independence.

The early ballad operas were not given by established opera companies, but by travelling stock companies. One such group, the Hallam Family, had over two hundred operas and musical plays in its repertory. These simple plays were given with English dialogue interspersed with folk tunes, and one of them included the new favorite, 'Yankee-Doodle.' These ballad operas reflected the topics of the day: *Tammany,* or *The Indian Chief, Columbus, Huzzah for the Constitution* and *The Fourth of July* were all popular at the time of the Revolution.

It was not until after the French Revolution, which elicited deep sympathy in the new Republic, that productions began to reflect the European flavor of opera. Since the end of the Eighteenth Century New Orleans was the

Maria Felicita Malibran

center of French opera, and various travelling troupes brought opera comique to the eastern seaboard cities. Italian opera buffa followed, with performances of Pergolesi's *Serva Padrona* and Paisiello's *Barber of Seville*, all given in English. In 1819, Rossini's *Barber of Seville* had its first performance, again in English. Facilities were usually so limited that the larger ensemble numbers were frequently omitted. European influence increased with the coming of the steamship when many travelling troupes arrived to tour the states. The famous Garcia family came in 1825; the Montressor troupe and Mozart's librettist Lorenzo da Ponte with his Italian company in 1832. There was new wealth in the expanding Republic and more money to spend on entertainment. This, and the desire to emulate European culture, led to a very rapid expansion of the local operatic scene. Garcia presented nine Italian operas at the Park Street Theatre during his first season of grand opera in New York. The year was 1825, and Garcia's daughter Malibran sang in the performances, which were given for the first time in the original language. A high price of two dollars was paid for a box seat to hear Malibran, one of the greatest singers ever to appear before an American public. Rapidly expanding New York became the home of Da Ponte's Italian company, for which a luxurious new opera auditorium was built. In 1844 the Palmos Opera House on Chambers Street opened its doors with Bellini's *I Puritani*, and interest ran so high that the Harlem Street Railroad ran a special horsecar as far north as 42nd Street to accommodate operagoers. Here, opera was first given in German. Three other theatres attest to the popularity of opera in New York: Richmond Hill,

Annie Louise Cary as Amneris

Giuseppe Mario

Niblo's Gardens, and Castle Garden. At Richmond Hill, which was once the home of Aaron Burr, Italian opera was given in 1832. English light opera was given at Niblo's until 1855, when German opera was performed, including performances of *Der Freischutz* and *Fidelio*. It was at Niblo's that Wagner was first given, *Tannhauser* in 1859. Castle Garden was first a fortress, then an immigration depot, and successively a restaurant, opera house, and aquarium. It was at Castle Garden on September 11, 1850, that Jenny Lind, the greatest coloratura of her time, sang under the management of Barnum. Seats for the concert sold at auction, one of them going for two hundred and twenty-five dollars. Six thousand people filled the hall, and hundreds of other New Yorkers, seated in boats, bobbed in the water surrounding the garden. Lind sang the Casta Diva from *Norma* in the original key of F, a feat never before accomplished in New York; and for her services that night it was rumored Barnum paid her $12,600, a fee which may be a permanent record.

Attempts at American opera were even less successful than opera in English in the face of the advancing tide of foreign opera. As trade and industry grew and the country expanded to the west, opera established itself in Chicago and San Francisco and other leading cities. But New York remained the center, and in 1854 The Academy of Music opened its doors at 14th Street and Irving Place. This opera house remained the leading gathering place for society until the opening of the Metropolitan Opera

Clara Louise Kellogg as Aida

House in 1883. Opera given in the language of its composition had become an integral part of the social life of the day, and as wealth and pretension increased, so did the aura surrounding the production of opera become more splendid. The famous singers of the day, Christine Nilsson, Campanini, Del Puente, Annie Louise Cary, Adelina Patti, Lucca, Sontag, Mario and Grisi, names which are memorable in the annals of opera, sang before adoring publics. The star system was at hand, and perhaps has never since been so luminous.

On Thanksgiving, 1859, at the Academy, singing *Lucia Di Lammermoor*, Adelina Patti made her debut in New York. She was seventeen years old, yet her phenomenal voice and perfect art astounded operagoers and overnight she became the acknowledged reigning prima donna. Patti left America in 1861 and did not return for twenty years, but her place was assumed by a new operatic star, the first American singer to become a popular diva, Clara Louise Kellogg. Miss Kellogg was a young lady of society, and it was considered highly improper for her to appear in works of so immoral a nature as *Rigoletto* and *La Traviata*, which had after all been banned in Boston. Nevertheless, her success was so great she was required to sing in *Faust* twenty-seven times in one season. Many memorable singers were heard in New York between the coming of Malibran and the brief three months which the tenor Mario and Mme. Giulia Grisi spent here, yet both earned enduring reputations.

With the astounding advances in science and industry, the coming of the telephone and telegraph, electricity, the gasoline engine and the tremendous growth of the railroads, a very rich new society arose. The Rockefellers, Morgans, Vanderbilts, and Goulds understandably wished for a larger opera house with more boxes in which to exhibit the ostentation of their wealth, and in 1883 these new tycoons built their own opera house, the Metropolitan.

New Yorkers enjoyed no monopoly on opera. As early as 1791 French opera had been successfully performed in New Orleans, but it was not until 1813 under the impresario John Davis that an imported opera company first performed there, at the new Theatre d'Orleans. Here operas of Rossini, Meyerbeer, Auber, and Donizetti were sung in French by Parisian singers. In 1859 Charles Boudousquie opened the French Opera House, where Adelina Patti made her debut in that city. New Orleans has preserved its tradition of opera into our own century.

In Philadelphia, as early as 1825, a company was performing *Der Freischutz* at the Chestnut Street Theatre in English. and two years later a touring company from New Orleans gave operas in French. In 1857 the Academy of Music was built. This fine old theatre, still in use today, was host to Lincoln, who heard opera there from a stage

Grisi and Lablache in "I Puritani"

Henriette Sontag

Ernesto Nicolini

Emma Abbott

box. The tradition of opera in Philadelphia embraces Italian, French, and German companies, the troupes of Maretzek, Strakosch, Grau, and such famous singers as Patti, Lucca, Nilsson, Lablache, and Nicolini.

At the Boston Federal Street Theatre in 1794, Charles Powell's company began a series of opera performances which endured several seasons. In 1854 The Boston Theatre opened, and provided the city with a fine auditorium seating over three thousand people which was ideally suited to the production of grand opera. For almost sixty years the theatre saw a succession of visiting companies.

La Sonnambula was given in Rice's Theatre, Chicago, on the 29th of July, 1850. It was the first opera professionally performed in the young town, and among the thirty thousand inhabitants of Chicago excitement ran high. The opera was avidly discussed but a longer season was cut short when the theatre burned on the second night. Three years later an Italian company gave *Lucia*, *La Sonnambula* and *Norma*. Sporadic seasons of opera followed until 1865, when a leading citizen built the Crosby Opera House which became the center of the city's operatic life for almost a decade. It was at Crosby's that Clara Louise Kellogg sang *The Daughter of the Regiment* before Generals Grant and Sherman and a distinguished audience.

San Francisco has a particularly vivid operatic history,

embracing such famous landmarks as the Adelphi Theatre, the Tivoli, and The Jenny Lind Theatre. As early as 1854 there were eleven opera houses in the town, all giving opera for the benefit of an enormous public.

Opera flourished in less cosmopolitan centers. Central City, Colorado, had an opera house in 1860, and the Central City Opera House, constructed in 1878, is still in use today. As early as 1820 Cleveland enjoyed an informal season of opera, and later years found many touring companies stopping there: the Parepa Rosa Opera Company, the Kellogg Company, and Emma Abbott and her Grand English Opera, among others. St. Louis, Atlanta, Baltimore and Cincinnati all enjoyed annual seasons of opera in the nineteenth century.

The vitality of European opera all but eclipsed native American attempts during these years, but the efforts of many, from the early Hallam Company down through troupes headed by Clara Louise Kellogg and Emma Abbott, kept alive the idea of opera in English and native opera. These groups and other touring companies were bringing opera, particularly European opera in the language of its composition, to every major city in the land by the end of the nineteenth century. With a relatively long history already behind it, opera was a flourishing institution in America.

L'Africaine

BY GIACOMO MEYERBEER
Libretto by Eugène Scribe

In Portugal during the age of discovery the Admiral Don Diego wishes his daughter Inez to forget her fiancé, the sailor Vasco da Gama who has long been absent on a voyage of discovery, and marry instead Don Pedro, the Councillor to the King. She remains true to Vasco, even though her father insists he must be dead, when suddenly the sailor returns with news of great discoveries. He has brought with him two of the inhabitants of a wonderful new country, Nelusko and Selika. When the displeased Don Diego doubts his stories, Vasco becomes enraged and speaks so violently against this injustice that he and the two captives are thrown in prison.

There Vasco is watched over by Selika who loves him. Nelusko, jealous of this love, attempts to stab Vasco but is prevented by Selika.

To free Vasco, Inez is forced to marry Don Pedro, who, after stealing the sailor's maps and charts and taking the two captives, sets sail in search of the unknown land. Vasco follows and comes on board in time to save Don Pedro's ship from a dangerous reef, but is put in irons. Indians attack the ship and take all on board prisoner, except Vasco who is saved by Selika, now revealed as the Queen of the Indian tribe.

The tribal high priest forces Selika to agree to kill all the crew except Vasco, who is so entranced by the beauty of Selika's country that he is prepared to remain forever and marry the queen. As the ceremony is about to be performed, Inez suddenly appears. The queen is convinced that Vasco loves Inez, and at the sacrifice of her own feelings, assists them to escape. As the ship bearing Vasco and Inez sails out to sea, Selika breathes the deadly fumes of the Mancanilla tree, preferring death to life without Vasco. She is joined in death by Nelusko, who in his grief also inhales the deadly blossoms.

Enrico Caruso as Vasco da Gama

Rosa Ponselle as Selika

Frederick Jagel as da Gama

Lillian Nordica as Selika

NOTES: WORLD PREMIERE: Grand Opera House, Paris, France, April 28, 1865. *Cast:* Vasco da Gama, Emilio Naudin; Selika, Marie Saxe; Inez, Marie Batteo; Nelusko, J. B. Faure; Don Pedro, M. Belval. AMERICAN PREMIERE: Academy of Music, New York, N. Y., December 1, 1865. METROPOLITAN OPERA PREMIERE (in German): December 7, 1888. *Cast:* Vasco da Gama, Perotti; Selika, Moran-Olden; Inez, Traubmann; Nelusko, Robinson; Don Pedro, Fischer.

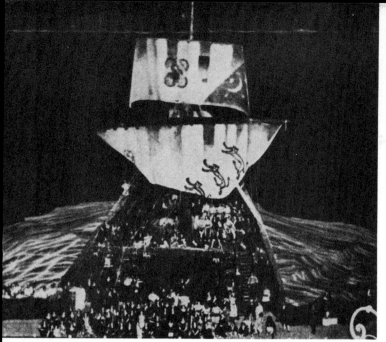

The ship of Don Pedro

Beniamino Gigli as da Gama

Johanna Gadski
as Selika

Giuseppe Danise
as Nelusko

The marriage ceremony of the Queen is about to be performed

Aida

BY GIUSEPPE VERDI

Libretto by Ghislanzoni.

In Ancient Egypt the soldier Rhadames is in love with the slave Aida, who unknown to him is the daughter of the King of Ethopia. Hearing he is to lead the invasion against the Ethiopians he hopes to place his triumphs at Aida's feet. The daughter of the Egyptian King, Amneris, is also deeply in love with Rhadames. She wonders at his joy and when Aida enters guesses the truth. The King formally invests Rhadames with command of the army and the soldier prepares for battle. Aida is torn between love for her native land and love for Rhadames.

Some time later Amneris is being adorned by her servants for the festival in honor of Rhadames' victories. She tricks Aida into confessing her love for Rhadames by telling her that he has been killed. In a great triumphal scene, Rhadames returns with many captives, among them Amonasro who is recognized as the Ethiopian King only by his daughter Aida. As a favor to Rhadames all the prisoners are released except Amonasro who is held as hostage, and the celebration ends when the Egyptian King bestows his daughter's hand upon Rhadames and declares him heir to the throne.

On the bank of the Nile Aida has come secretly at night for a last meeting with Rhadames but is intercepted by her father who persuades her to betray to him the movements of the Egyptian army. He hides when Rhadames appears. Aida begs her lover to escape with her and learns of the army's movements. Amonasro overhears the information, reveals his identity, and urges Rhadames to side with the Ethiopians. Amneris, praying in the nearby temple, overhears the conversation and enters to denounce Rhadames, who is taken prisoner as Aida and her father escape.

Rhadames is tried and sentenced to be buried alive, but Amneris seeks to save him if he will renounce Aida. He refuses, and when he is sealed in the tomb he finds Aida who has come to die with him. They perish together while the unhappy Princess kneels in prayer above the tomb.

Enrico Caruso as Rhadames and Adamo Didur as Ramfis in the consecration scene as enacted on November 16, 1908. This marked the debuts of Arturo Toscanini as conductor and Emmy Destinn as Aida at the Metropolitan Opera House.

Emmy Destinn as Aida and Antonio Scotti as Amonasro.

The banks of the Nile where Aida (Zinka Milanov) begs her lover, Rhadames (Mario Del Monaco) to escape with her while Amonasro (George London) urges him to side with the Ethiopians.

Rhadames returns in triumph and receives the hand of the Egyptian King's daughter in marriage.

NOTES: WORLD PREMIERE: Khedive Theatre, Cairo, Egypt, December 24, 1871. *Cast:* Aida, Pozzoni; Amneris, Grossi; Rhadames, Mongini; Amonasro, Stella; Ramfis, Medini; King, Costa. AMERICAN PREMIERE: Academy of Music, New York City, November 25, 1873. *Cast:* Aida, Ottavia Torriani; Amneris, Annie Louise Cary; Rhadames, Italo Campanini; King, Giovanni Scolara; Amonasro, Victor Maurel; Ramfis, Nannetti. METROPOLITAN OPERA PREMIERE (in German): November 12, 1886. *Cast:* Aida, Theresa Herbert-Forster; Amneris, Marianne Brandt; Rhadames, Carl Zobel; Amonasro, Adolf Robinson; King, George Sieglitz.

◄

Nellie Melba first sang Aida
in America at Philadelphia,
January 13, 1898

Amneris (Marjorie Lawrence)
with her slaves

Enrico Caruso
as Rhadames

Ottavia Torriani,
first Aida in America

Italo Campanini
first to sing Rhadames
in America

Clara Louise Kellogg,
one of the first American Aidas

Amneris (Thorborg) curses Ramfis (Pinza)
for sentencing Rhadames to death

Claudia Muzio
as Aida

Aida ballet. Photo taken during performance at Met opening night
(Dec. 22nd) of 1934-35 season

The lovers
are entombed

Giovanni Zenatello
as Rhadames

Richard Bonelli
as Amonasro

Blanche Thebom
as Amneris

Eleanor De Cisneros
as Amneris

Lawrence Tibbett
as Amonasro

Rose Bampton first
sang Amneris at Met
March 24, 1933

Mario Del Monaco
as Rhadames

Kathleen Howard
as Amneris

Louise Homer made her debut
at Met December 22, 1900
singing Amneris

Lillian Nordica
as Aida

Edward Johnson
as Rhadames

Elena Nikolaidi
as Amneris

Nicolo Zerola, Italian tenor,
who sang Rhadames with
Manhattan Opera Company

Pasquale Amato
as Amonasro

[18]

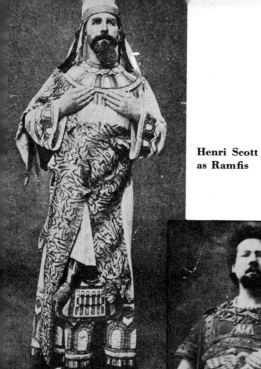

Henri Scott
as Ramfis

Marie Brema, English
contralto (real name
Minny Fehrman),
as Amneris

George London
as Amonasro

Leo Slezak
as Rhadames

ra Barbieri
nneris

Pol Plancon,
French bass, first sang
Ramfis at Met,
December 8, 1894

Rosa Raisa, Polish soprano, made her
American debut November 28, 1913, as Aida
at Auditorium, Chicago, with
Chicago Opera Company

Beniamino Gigli
as Rhadames

Bruna Castagna made her Met debut
as Amneris, March 2, 1936

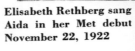

Robert Merri
as Amonasi

Elisabeth Rethberg sang
Aida in her Met debut
November 22, 1922

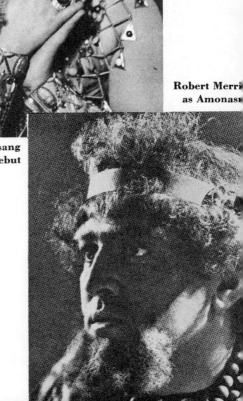

Emmy Destinn made
her Met debut November
16, 1908, as Aida

Emma Eames as Aida

Albert Saleza, French tenor, first
sang Rhadames at the Met,
February 1, 1901

Giovanni Martinelli as Rhadames

Alceste

BY CHRISTOPH WILLIBALD GLUCK
Libretto by Raniero da Calzabigi

Admetus, the legendary King of Thessaly, is mortally ill. Despite the prayers of his anguished people, the Gods will not spare his life. Alceste, the King's wife, prays with the people for her husband's recovery at the steps of the temple. They beseech the Oracle to give them encouragement. Instead, the Oracle declares that Admetus must die unless there can be found among his people one who will be willing to die in his place. The terror-stricken people flee from the temple leaving Alceste alone in her sorrow. In anguish she swears to the Gods that she herself will make the supreme sacrifice in order to save her husband.

The joyous people assemble at the palace to rejoice over the King's dramatic recovery, unaware that it is Alceste herself who must now die. Admetus questions his wife about his miraculous recovery and, unable to hold back her own tears, she turns aside from his gaze. Suspicious, Admetus insists on knowing the name of the friend who is so devoted he is willing to sacrifice his life for him. Alceste at length admits it is she herself who must now die. The horrified king implores the Gods to strike him dead and save Alceste, but it is to no avail. She must fulfil the prediction of the Oracle of Apollo. Mournfully bidding a last farewell, Alceste begins her trip to Hades.

Sustained by her faith and love for Admetus, Alceste passes through the terrors of the underworld. Admetus follows her to the gates of Hades, where he begs her to give up her resolve to die for him. She remains adamant, and the anguished king challenges the Gods to take his wife. Suddenly Apollo appears, praising the courageous Admetus, and allows Alceste to return to life. Joyously they come back to their kingdom to be greeted by the jubilant people.

NOTES: WORLD PREMIERE: Vienna Burghtheater, December 26, 1767. *Cast:* Alceste, Antonia Bernasconi; Admetus, Giuseppe Tibaldi; High Priest, Laschi; Voice of Apollo, Laschi. American Premiere: Wellesley College, Mass., March 11, 1938. *Cast:* Alceste, Dorothy Baker; Admetus; Joseph Lautner; High Priest, Joseph Haroutunian; Voice of Apollo, David McAlister. Metropolitan Opera Premiere: January 24, 1941. *Cast:* Alceste, Marjorie Lawrence; Admetus, Rene Maison; High Priest, Leonard Warren; Voice of Apollo, Arthur Kent; Evander, Alessio De Paolis.

Celebration of the lovers' reunion

Brian Sullivan as Admetus

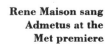

Kirsten Flagstad as Alceste

Rene Maison sang Admetus at the Met premiere

Marjorie Lawrence sang Alceste at Met premiere, January 24, 1941

[23]

Avito comes for a last farewell to Fiora who
lies in state in the crypt of the castle

L'Amore Dei Tre Re
(The Love of Three Kings)

BY ITALO MONTEMEZZI
Libretto by Sem Benelli

During the middle ages, after he has conquered the Italian province in which the story takes place, the blind King Archibaldo has married his son Manfredo to the native Princess Fiora, who is a hostage of the wars. Fiora hates her husband, and loves instead Avito, a native prince to whom she was engaged before the war separated them. When the king's son Manfredo goes to war, the two lovers have many opportunities together, for one of Avito's henchmen is a guide to the blind king and manages to smuggle Avito in and out of the castle. The king often interrupts the lovers and suspects his daughter-in-law but cannot establish the identity of her lover.

Manfredo comes back from the wars on a brief visit and pleads passionately for his wife's affections. She finally yields to him, promising to wave a scarf from the castle walls when he returns to his soldiers. Determined to be true to her husband, she now spurns the attentions of Avito when he appears after Manfredo has gone, but little by little her resolve falters and finally she calls Avito back. During the love scene which follows the blind king enters and forces Fiora to admit her guilt, whereupon he strangles her.

Meanwhile Manfredo, not seeing his wife upon the battlements as she had promised, fears she is in danger and returns to find her dying, killed by her father-in-law for her unfaithfulness.

Deep in the crypt of the castle Fiora lies in state, and the king has placed poison on her lips hoping thereby to punish the man who was her lover. Avito comes for a last farewell, kisses the fatal lips, and slowly dies. At this moment Manfredo enters to learn from the dying Avito that he was Fiora's lover. Throwing himself upon the corpse in grief, Manfredo also kisses her lips, and when the old blind king enters to enjoy his vengeance on Fiora's lover, he finds that his son too has become a victim of his rage.

The princess Fiora
embraces her lover

Manfredo (Pasquale Amato) realizes his wife
Fiora (Lucrezia Bori) is dead by the hands
of his father Archibaldo (Adamo Didur)

Edward Johnson sang
Avito in his Met
debut, Nov. 16, 1922

Mary Garden
as Fiora

Grace Moore as
Fiora

Lucrezia Bori who was
the first to sing Fiora
in America,
January 2, 1914

Virgilio Lazzari
as Archibaldo

NOTES: WORLD PREMIERE: La Scala, Milan, Italy, April 10, 1913.
Cast: Archibaldo, Nazzareno de Angelis; Manfredo, Carlo Galeffi;
Fiora, Luisa Villani. AMERICAN PREMIERE: Metropolitan Opera
House, New York, N. Y., January 2, 1914. *Cast:* Archibaldo, Adamo
Didur; Manfredo, Pasquale Amato; Fiora, Lucrezia Bori.

Helen Jepson as
Fiora with Armand
Tokatyan as Avito

La Boheme

BY GIACOMO PUCCINI
Libretto by Giuseppe Giacosa
and Luigi Illica

Four starving Bohemians in a Paris garret manage to laugh and joke away their misfortunes. One of them has finally sold a composition and there is food and drink. During the celebration the landlord appears for the rent but soon forgets his mission under the influence of the wine they force on him. Schaunard, Colline, and Marcello depart for a party in the Latin Quarter leaving the poet Rodolfo alone to work. He is soon interrupted by the appearance of Mimi, a neighbor who has come to borrow a light. They tell each other of their experiences and soon confess to love at first sight and go off happily to join Rodolfo's friends.

It is Christmas Eve in the Latin Quarter and the four Bohemians and Rodolfo's new-found love are celebrating when Musetta, an old flame of Marcello's, comes into the square with Alcindoro, a rich old man. In order to be with Marcello Musetta pretends her shoes are too tight and sends Alcindoro after another pair. When the bill is presented the happy group find they haven't the money to pay, but Musetta solves the difficulty by charging it all to Alcindoro, who returns to receive the bill just as the others disappear happily down the street.

At a customs gate near the edge of Paris Mimi has come to find Marcello and tell him of the many quarrels she has had with Rodolfo and that he has left her despite how much she loves him. When Rodolfo appears Mimi hides and overhears him tell Marcello that she is dying of consumption. Mimi is overcome by a fit of coughing and the two lovers become reconciled as Marcello and Musetta, who now appears from the local inn, quarrel loudly over her flirting.

In the cold garret Marcello and Rodolfo are trying to work despite the memories of their unhappy love affairs when Schaunard and Colline arrive and prepare supper. The gaiety is interrupted when Musetta enters with the dying Mimi. When the others go for money and medicine Rodolfo and Mimi dream of their past happiness. The others arrive as Mimi dies in the heartbroken Rodolfo's arms.

Christmas Eve in the street outside the cafe in the Latin Quarter

At the customs gate near the edge of Paris, Mimi and Rodolfo are reconciled

Rodolfo tells Marcello that Mimi is fatally ill with consumption while she listens behind a tree

NOTES: WORLD PREMIERE: Teatro Reggio, Turin, Italy, February 1, 1896. *Cast:* Mimi, Cesira Ferrani; Musetta, Camilla Possini; Rodolfo, Evan Gorga; Marcello, Tieste Wilmant; Schaunard, Antonio Pini-Corsi; Colline, Mazzara. AMERICAN PREMIERE: Los Angeles Theatre, Los Angeles, Calif., October 14, 1897. *Cast:* Mimi, Linda Montanari; Musetta, Cleopatra Vicini; Rodolfo, Giuseppe Agostini; Marcello, Caesar Cioni; Schaunard, Luigi Francesconi; Colline, Vittorio Girardi. FIRST NEW YORK CITY PERFORMANCE AT WALLACK'S THEATRE, May 16, 1898, by a company called the Milan Royal Opera Company of La Scala and formerly known as the Baggetto Grand Italian Opera Company. *Cast:* Mimi, Linda Montanari; Musetta, Cleopatra Vincini, Rodolfo, Giuseppe Agostini; Marcello, Luigi Francesconi; Schaunard, Giovanni Scolari. METROPOLITAN OPERA HOUSE PREMIERE: December 26, 1900. *Cast:* Mimi, Nellie Melba; Musetta, Signorina Occhiolini; Rodolfo, Albert Saleza; Marcello, Giuseppe Campanari; Schaunard, Charles Gilibert; Colline, Marcel Journet.

The Bohemians with Colline (Ezio Pinza) and Mimi (Lucrezia Bori) celebrate at the Cafe Momus

The frail Mimi, near death, is comforted by Rodolfo

John McCormack
as Rodolfo

Alessandro Bonci
as Rodolfo

Alma Gluck
as Mimi

Ferruccio Tagliavini
made his debut at the
Met singing Rodolfo,
Jan. 10, 1947

Frances Alda
as Mimi

Thomas Chalmers
as Marcello

Victoria De Los Angeles as Mimi

Fritzi Scheff sang Musetta at the Met for the first time, Jan. 11, 1901

Giuseppe Agostini sang Rodolfo at the American premiere of the opera

Antonio Scotti as Marcello

Grace Moore as Mimi, made her debut at the Met, Feb. 7, 1928

Mario Sammarco
as Marcello

Claudia Muzio
as Mimi

Patrice Munsel
as Musetta

Jarmila Novotna made
her Met debut as
Mimi, January 5, 1940

Bidu Sayao
as Mimi

Brenda Lewis
as Musetta

Geraldine Farrar
as Mimi

Enrico Caruso
as Rodolfo

Lucrezia Bori
as Mimi

Jussi Bjoerling made his
Met debut November 24, 1938, as Rodolfo

Richard Bonelli
as Marcello

Count Almaviva serenades Rosina
while Figaro watches

The Barber of Seville

BY GIOACCHINO ANTONIO ROSSINI
Libretto by Cesare Sterbini

In 17th Century Seville a Dr. Bartolo wishes to marry his ward Rosina for her money, and is assisted by her music teacher, Basilio, in guarding her from all other suitors. Despite their attempts Rosina and Count Almaviva love each other, and he seeks an opportunity of getting to see her as he serenades her beneath her balcony. The town barber Figaro suggests the count disguise himself as a drunken soldier and get into the house that way. Rosina knows the count only as 'Lindoro, a poor student.'

Inside the house Rosina has just written a love-note to her 'Lindoro,' and Dr. Bartolo is suspicious. Basilio suggests they make the character of the Count unsavory by spreading innuendoes against his character so that he will leave Seville. After they have left, Figaro comes to plead for 'Lindoro' and Rosina gives him the letter she has just written. Disguised as a drunken soldier, the Count enters with a letter of his own for Rosina, and Dr. Bartolo

bustles in to order his arrest. The officers, unknown to Dr. Bartolo, quickly release the drunken soldier on learning his true identity.

In the music room, the Count now appears as a music teacher, saying that Basilio is ill and that he has been sent in his stead. While the music lesson continues, Figaro shaves Bartolo in order to distract him while the lovers plan an elopement. Basilio, the real music teacher, suddenly arrives, but is bribed to pretend to be sick. The lovers' plans are spoiled when Bartolo hurries off to get the marriage contracts in his own favor drawn up by the notary public. When Basilio and the notary arrive, the Count and Figaro again bribe Basilio and the contract is made out in the Count's favor. But the outwitted Dr. Bartolo is somewhat appeased by being allowed to keep Rosina's money, and all ends happily.

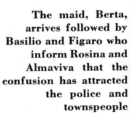

The maid, Berta, arrives followed by Basilio and Figaro who inform Rosina and Almaviva that the confusion has attracted the police and townspeople

NOTES: WORLD PREMIERE: Argentina Theatre, Rome, Italy, February 5, 1816. *Cast:* Rosina, Giorgi-Righetti; Figaro, Luigi Zamboni; Almaviva, Manuel Garcia; Bartolo, Botticelli. AMERICAN PREMIERE (in English): Park Theatre, New York City, May 17, 1819. *Cast:* Rosina, Catharine Lessugg; Figaro, Spiller; Almaviva, Thomas Phillippe; Bartolo, John Barnes. FIRST OPERA TO BE SUNG IN ITALIAN IN NEW YORK AT THE PARK THEATRE, November 29, 1825. *Cast:* Rosina, Maria Felicita Garcia; Almaviva, Manuel Garcia, Sr.; Figaro, Manuel Garcia, Jr.; Bartolo, Rosich. METROPOLITAN OPERA PREMIERE: November 23, 1883. *Cast:* Rosina, Marcella Sembrich; Figaro, Giuseppe del Puente; Almaviva, Roberto Stagno; Bartolo, Baldassare Corsini.

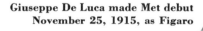

Marcella Sembrich as Rosina. She sang her farewell to the operatic stage in America at the Met, Feb. 6, 1909

Giuseppe De Luca made Met debut November 25, 1915, as Figaro

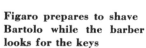

Figaro prepares to shave Bartolo while the barber looks for the keys

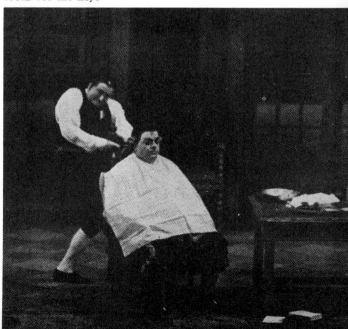

[33]

Titta Ruffo, who made Met debut
January 19, 1922, as Figaro

Alice Nielson as Rosina

John Charles Thomas
first sang Figaro at Met
January 22, 1938

Jerome Hines as
Don Basilio

[34]

Nino Martini sang
his first Almaviva
January 17, 1939,
at the Met

Feodor Chaliapin
as Don Basilio

Salvatore Baccaloni as
Dr. Bartolo with
Norman Cordon as
Don Basilio

Adelina Patti made
her last appearance at
Met April 9, 1892,
as Rosina

Amelita Galli-Curci
as Rosina

Lily Pons
as Rosina

Patrice Munsel
as Rosina

Charles Hackett made his Met
debut, January 31, 1919,
as Almaviva

Mario Sammarco
as Figaro

**Nellie Melba
as Rosina**

**Ezio Pinza
as Don Basilio**

**Cesare Siepi
as Don Basilio**

**Ferruccio Tagliavini
as Almaviva**

Amid great pomp
Boris accepted the throne

The death of Boris

Adamo Didur who sang the first Boris in
America at the Met, March 19, 1913

Boris Godunov

MUSIC AND LIBRETTO BY MODEST PETROVICH MOUSSORGSKY

Russia, 1600. The regent Boris Godunov, hoping to succeed to the throne left vacant by the death of Ivan the Terrible's son, has secretly murdered the rightful heir, his nephew Dimitri. Pretending no desire for the crown, he has gone to a convent to expiate his sin, but his hirelings compel the populace by threats and violence to beg Boris to accept.

In a cell in the Convent of Miracles an old monk Pimen tells the story of Dimitri's death to Grigori, a young man of Dimitri's age, who resolves to spread the report that Dimitri still lives (in his person) and thus usurp the crown for himself.

Amid great pomp Boris accepts the throne and is crowned.

Grigori escapes into Lithuania where he hopes to raise an army after barely escaping arrest at the frontier.

In the Palace the new Czar is a prey to fears and remorse, heightened when he learns the people, believing Dimitri still lives, are in revolt. He begins to wonder if Dimitri's ghost has actually risen against him.

In Poland the fires of Grigori's ambition are fanned by the lovely Marina who finds it in her and her country's interest to help Grigori play his role.

In the Kromy Forest the disaffection of the peasants is whipped up by the appearance of the pretender and the people follow Grigori in revolt.

The Duma gathers at the palace to plan measures against the uprising, and hear an insinuation that Boris has murdered Dimitri, but action is cut short by the entrance of the Czar. Pimen comes forth to tell of a dream in which a blind man was restored to sight by a miracle at Dimitri's tomb. Boris listens with growing horror and his mania increases until all realize he is dying. Alone with his son, he bids a pathetic farewell and dies in great agony. The opera ends abruptly, the fate of Grigori's rebellion unknown.

NOTES: WORLD PREMIERE: Imperial Opera House, St. Petersburg, Russia, February 8, 1874. *Cast:* Boris, Melinkov; Feodor, Krutikov; Marina, Julia Feodorivina Platanova; Prince Schouisky, Vasillev II; Dimitri, Kamissarjevsky. AMERICAN PREMIERE (in Italian): Metropolitan Opera House, New York, N. Y., March 19, 1913. *Cast:* Boris, Adamo Didur; Feodor, Anna Case; Marina, Louise Homer; Prince Schouisky, Angelo Bada; Dimitri, Paul Althouse.

▶

Feodor Chaliapin, who always sang in Russian, made his first appearance as Boris in America at the Met, Dec. 9, 1921

Jeanne Maubourg as
the Innkeeper with
Andres de Segurola as
Varlaam

Anna Case as Feodor with
Adamo Didur as Boris

In the Kromy forest, Dimitri is
hailed by Varlaam and crowd

Louise Homer, as Marina, with
Paul Althouse who made his Met
debut as Dimitri, March 19, 1913

Alexander Kipnis first sang Boris
at Met, February 13, 1943

Cesare Siepi
as Boris

Scene with American premiere cast including
Adamo Didur and Angelo Bada

Irra Petina as
Feodor with Pinza as Boris

Nicola Rossi-Lemeni
as Boris

Ezio Pinza sang Boris at Met
for the first time March 7, 1939

George London
as Boris

Carmen is surrounded by soldiers after the stabbing of her fellow worker

Carmen

BY GEORGES BIZET
Libretto by Henri Meilhac and Ludovic Halévy

Seville in 1800. Soldiers wait in the hot afternoon for the guard to change. A simple country girl Micaela comes with a message from his mother for one of them, Don José, who appears with the guard relief. Girls emerge from the cigarette factory where they work and the soldiers flirt with them. The gypsy Carmen is the most admired but she spurns all except Don José who is indifferent to her, until she throws her flower at his feet. After the girls re-enter the factory Micaela brings José the letter and he is about to throw away Carmen's flower when screams are heard in the factory. Carmen has stabbed one of the girls in a fight and is arrested, but escapes through Jose's intervention after they agree to meet later.

Gypsies and smugglers celebrate at an inn where the bullfighter Escamillo is welcomed. When José comes Carmen urges him to join the smugglers. He refuses, but when his superior appears and orders him out and a sword fight ensues, José joins Carmen and the smugglers as they escape into the mountains.

In the mountain hide-away Carmen's affections now turn toward the toreador and the two jealous rivals fight with daggers, but are separated by the others. Escamillo leaves for the bullring, inviting the others to follow. Micaela comes to urge José to return to his dying mother and he finally leaves with her, bitterly cursing Carmen.

Crowds gather outside the arena for the bullfight. Carmen promises herself to Escamillo and the crowds swarm into the arena, except for Carmen who is prevented by the enraged José, still desperately in love with her. In a violent quarrel he stabs her dead, as the toreador comes victoriously from the arena.

NOTES: WORLD PREMIERE: Opéra Comique, Paris, France, March 3, 1875. *Cast:* Don José, Paul Lhérie; Escamillo, Jacques Bouhy; Micaela, Mme. Chapuy; Carmen, Cellestine Galli-Marié. AMERICAN PREMIERE: Academy of Music, New York City, October 23, 1878. *Cast:* Don José, Italo Campanini; Escamillo, Giuseppe del Puente; Micaela, Mme. Sinico; Carmen, Minnie Hauk. METROPOLITAN OPERA PREMIERE (in Italian): January 9, 1884. *Cast:* Don José, Italo Campanini; Escamillo, Giuseppe del Puente; Micaela, Alwina Vallerie; Carmen, Zelia Trebelli. Presented in German at the Metropolitan Opera House November 25, 1885.

The smugglers try to
persuade Carmen to
join them

Carmen reads a
prophecy of death in
the cards

Police and populace close in on
Don José at Carmen's murder

Carmen's death outside
the bull ring

**Mario Del Monaco
as Don José**

**Italo Campanini,
first to sing Don José
in America**

**Rise Stevens
as Carmen**

**Minnie Hauk,
first American Carmen**

**Ezio Pinza
as Escamillo**

**Giuseppe Del Puente,
first to sing
Escamillo in America**

Maria Gay made her
Met debut as Carmen,
December 3, 1908

Caruso as Don José which he first sang
at the Met March 5, 1906

Geraldine Farrar and Enrico Caruso
as Carmen and Don José

Frank Guarrera,
Philadelphia baritone,
as Escamillo

[45]

Marguerite Sylva
as Carmen

Licia Albanese
as Micaela

Lucien Muratore
as Don José

Beniamino Gigli
as Don José

Edmond Clément
as Don José

Olive Fremstad sang
her first Carmen
at the Met
November 25, 1904

Rosa Ponselle sang her first Carmen at the Met
December 27, 1935

Emmy Destinn
as Carmen

George London
as Escamillo

Emma Trentini
as Frasquita

Marcella Sembrich
as Carmen

George Baklanoff
as Escamillo

Myrna Sharlow
as Carmen

Ralph Errole
as Don José

Alice Gentle as Carmen. She began
her operatic career
in the chorus of
Manhattan Opera Company

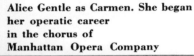

Ramon Vinay made his debut
at the Met, February 22, 1946,
as Don José

Gladys Swarthout
as Carmen

Jeanne Gerville-Reache
as Carmen

Pol Plancon as
Escamillo

Giovanni Zenatello
as Don José

Emma Calvé
in her most famous role, Carmen,
which she first sang at the Met
December 20, 1893

Zelie De Lussan

José Mardones
as Escamillo

Marguerite D'Alvarez
as Carmen

Mary Garden
as Carmen

Edward Johnson
as Don José

ale Amato
camillo

Marcel Journet
as Escamillo

Andres De Segurola
as Escamillo

Dusolina Giannini
as Carmen

Maria Jeritza
as Carmen

Geraldine Farrar sang
her first Carmen at
the Met
November 19, 1914

Cavalleria Rusticana

BY PIETRO MASCAGNI

Libretto by Giovanni Targioni-Tazetti and Guido Menasci

In a poor Sicilian village a young soldier Turiddu has returned from service to find Lola, the girl he loves, already married to Alfio, another villager. Another village girl, Santuzza is in love with Turiddu but fears he desperately wants to return to Lola. The peasants and townspeople crowd into the small church on Easter morning, except for Santuzza who tells her sad story to Turiddu's mother. The mother is greatly upset but can suggest no way to help the poor girl, and finally goes on into the church, leaving Santuzza alone when Turiddu appears with Lola. She begs him to return to her but he refuses to listen and pushes past her into the church with Lola. The embittered Santuzza then tells Lola's husband of his wife's unfaithfulness, and he threatens to kill Turiddu.

After the services the villagers, Turiddu, and Lola come out of the church. At his mother's wine shop across the square Turiddu sings a drinking song and invites Alfio to join him in a drink. The enraged husband instead challenges Turiddu to a duel by biting his ear, in the Sicilian fashion. Turiddu takes up the challenge. Alone with his mother he begs her to look after Santuzza, whom he now regrets having wronged. The two rivals go off to a field outside of town, and soon peasants rush back to the square with news that Alfio has slain Turiddu.

NOTES: WORLD PREMIERE: Teatro Constanzi, Rome, Italy, May 17, 1890. *Cast:* Santuzza, Gemma Bellincioni; Lola, A. Galli; Turiddu, Roberto Stagno; Alfio, Salassa; Lucia, F. Casali. AMERICAN PREMIERE: Grand Opera House, Philadelphia, Pennsylvania, September 9, 1891. *Cast:* Santuzza, Selma Kort-Krongold; Lola, Helen Dudley Campbell; Turiddu, Albert L. Guille; Alfio, Giuseppe del Puente; Lucia, Jennie Teal. METROPOLITAN OPERA PREMIERE: December 30, 1891. *Cast:* Santuzza, Emma Eames; Lola, Giulia Ravogli; Turiddu, Fernando Valero; Alfio, Edoardo Camera; Lucia, Matilde Bauermeister.

Enrico Caruso as Turiddu and Emmy Destinn as Santuzza

The Sicilian villagers congregate
in the square after church

Mario Chamlee
as Turiddu

Francesco Tamagno
as Turiddu

Emma Eames
as Santuzza

[53]

The lovers swear their girls are true

Cosi Fan Tutte

BY WOLFGANG AMADEUS MOZART
Libretto by Lorenzo da Ponte

In eighteenth century Naples two young men, Guglielmo and Ferrando, who firmly believe in the virtue and chastity of their respective lady friends, Fiordiligi and Dorabella, accept the wager of their elderly cynical friend Alfonso who bets that he can prove the infidelity of the two ladies in question.

While praising their absent lovers, Fiordiligi and Dorabella are surprised in their garden by Alfonso, who reports that Guglielmo and Ferrando have been ordered off to war. Presently the men themselves come to say farewell. After their departure, the grief of the ladies is hysterical. And they particularly resent the cynicism of the maid, Despina, who has a thing or two to say about the faithfulness of soldiers away from home. Meanwhile, Alfonso has bribed Despina to introduce Guglielmo and Ferrando, disguised as amorous Albanians, to the unsuspecting ladies. The men are very pleased with their fiancées when their romantic overtures are repulsed, and Fiordiligi and Dorabella stalk off indignantly.

Alone in their garden the mournful sisters are surprised when Guglielmo and Ferrando, still disguised, stagger in and pretend suicide, apparently in the throes of desperate passion. There are indications that the ladies are softening. The men recover, and at the urging of Despina, Dorabella decides to flirt with Guglielmo, while Ferrando and Fiordiligi stroll off together. Later, the two men relate the success each has had with the other's fiancée, and they are naturally quite disturbed.

On their terrace the ladies agree with Despina that love is indeed powerful, and when the two suitors again threaten suicide, they yield to their passions.

At a wedding feast where the ladies are about to unite with their 'Albanians,' Alfonso suddenly announces the arrival of Guglielmo and Ferrando, back from the wars. In the confusion Fiordiligi and Dorabella push their grooms into another room. Presently they reappear as Guglielmo and Ferrando. Amid the apologies the sweethearts are properly reunited. Blaming Alfonso for everything, they decide that, philosophically, perhaps all can be forgiven.

NOTES: WORLD PREMIERE: Court Theatre, Vienna, January 26, 1790. *Cast:* Fiordiligi, Adriana Ferrarese del Bene; Dorabella, Louise Villeneuve; Despina, Dorotea Bussani; Ferrando, Vincenzo Calvesi; Guglielmo, Francesco Benucci; Don Alfonso, Francesco Bussani. AMERICAN PREMIERE: Metropolitan Opera House, New York, March 24, 1922. *Cast:* Fiordiligi, Florence Easton; Dorabella, Frances Peralta; Despina, Lucrezia Bori; Ferrando, George Meador; Guglielmo, Giuseppe DeLuca; Don Alfonso, Adamo Didur.

Blanche Thebom
as Dorabella

Florence Easton who sang
Fiordiligi in the first performance
in America at the Met,
March 24, 1922

Patrice Munsel
as Despina

Eleanor Steber
as Fiordiligi

In a seaside garden Guglielmo (Frank Guarrera) and
Ferrando (Richard Tucker) bid Fiordiligi (Eleanor
Steber) and Dorabella (Blanche Thebom)
farewell as Don Alfonso (John Brownlee) starts
his plotting

The notary arrives for the wedding feast

Marie accompanies herself on the drums while she sings a song

The Daughter of the Regiment

BY GAETANO DONIZETTI
Libretto by Bayard and Jules H. Vernoy

During a lull in one of the local wars, the peasants living in the Mountains of the Swiss Tyrol, with their wives and children, are praying for victory. Along the road comes Sergeant Sulpice, an old grumbler, and behind him is a pretty girl in uniform, Marie, the daughter of the regiment, who was found on the battlefield when she was a child and has been brought up in the regiment as the spoiled darling of the grenadiers. Marie amuses herself and the peasants by accompanying herself on the drums while she sings a song. Marie is in love with a young man who saved her from falling over a cliff, but the grenadiers have decreed that only a grenadier shall have her as wife. Suddenly Tonio is dragged in and accused of spying, but Marie pleads for him, as he is the young man she is in love with. Wishing to be near Marie, he decides to enlist in the regiment.

The Marquise from a nearby castle examines some papers which were found on Marie when she was discovered as a baby on the battlefield, and declares that Marie is her niece and must henceforth live in the castle. Tonio has become a soldier for nothing. And poor Marie goes off to live in the castle with her new aunt.

Though Marie is learning to dance the minuet and to sing classical airs, and is presently to be married to a local heir, her irrepressible good spirits are hard to dampen. With Sergeant Sulpice she amuses herself singing the old regimental tunes, and the grenadiers troop in, with Tonio at their head, for he has been made a captain for bravery. Sulpice can see no logical reason why Marie should not marry Tonio instead of the nobleman, but the aunt confesses that Marie is her own daughter, born out of wedlock. Not wishing to disappoint her mother, Marie agrees to marry the nobleman.

As the wedding guests assemble for the signing of the marriage contract, Marie scandalizes them by singing fondly of her childhood in the regiment. The Marquise is moved by her daughter's happy memories, and decides that she must marry Tonio after all.

NOTES: WORLD PREMIERE: Opera Comique, Paris, France, February 11, 1840. AMERICAN PREMIERE: New Orleans Opera House, New Orleans, Louisiana, March 7, 1843. METROPOLITAN OPERA PREMIERE: January 6, 1902. *Cast:* Marie, Marcella Sembrich; Tonio, Thomas Salignac; Sulpice, Charles Gilibert.

Lily Pons as Marie

Louis D'Angelo
as Sulpice

John McCormack
as Tonio

Frieda Hempel as Marie

The Marquise decides that Marie must marry Tonio after all

Marie goes off to
live in a castle with
her new aunt

The Cloister Gardens of the Monastery

Don Carlos

BY GIUSEPPE VERDI
Libretto by Joseph Mery and Camille du Locle

Don Carlos, the son of Philip II, King of Spain, is deeply in love with the beautiful daughter of the king of France, Elizabeth de Valois. But reasons of state compel her to marry, instead of the man she loves, his father Philip II. Confiding his love for his stepmother to Rodrigo, Don Carlos is urged to leave the Spanish court to avoid trouble, and therefore asks the Queen to obtain his father's permission to join the Flemings in their struggle against the Spaniards. The passion between the two lovers returns in greater intensity as a result of their secret meeting.

The King, however, wishes the Spanish tyrants to win a victory and his son's strange request angers him. Father and son are further estranged.

The Princess Eboli learns that the queen still loves Don Carlos, and jealously informs Philip of that fact. The unhappy monarch is angered and embittered, thinking of his unhappy condition and his unloving wife. On the advice of the Grand Inquisitor he has Don Carlos arrested and thrown into jail. The Princess Eboli repents her act and confesses to the queen, who orders her from the court. The Princess is left griefstricken and alone.

Rodrigo visits the prince in prison and is shot by friends of the king who suspect him of giving aid to the Flemings. He dies in Don Carlos' arms.

After being freed Don Carlos keeps a tryst with Elizabeth at the monastery of St. Just where the king surprises the lovers together. The prince is handed over to the Inquisition and led away to death.

The Square before the Cathedral

Richard Tucker as Don Carlos

Feodor Chaliapin as Philip II

**Nicola Rossi-Lemeni
as Don Carlos**

**Blanche Thebom
as Princess Eboli**

Cesare Siepi as Philip II

NOTES: WORLD PREMIERE (in French): Paris Opera House, Paris, France, March 11, 1867. *Cast:* Philip II, Obin; Don Carlos, Morera; Rodrigo, Jean Baptiste Faure; Grand Inquisitor, David; Elizabeth, Marie Sass; Princess Eboli, Gueymard. AMERICAN PREMIERE: Academy of Music, New York City, April 12, 1877. *Cast:* Philip II, Dal Negro; Don Carlos, Celada; Rodrigo, Bertolasi; Grand Inquisitor, Gorini; Elizabeth, Marie Palmieri; Princess Eboli, Bastelli. METROPOLITAN OPERA PREMIERE: December 23, 1920. *Cast:* Philip II, Adamo Didur; Don Carlos, Giovanni Martinelli; Rodrigo, Giuseppe DeLuca; Grand Inquisitor, Louis D'Angelo; Elizabeth, Rosa Ponselle; Princess Eboli, Margarete Matzenauer.

Delia Rigal as Elizabeth

Don Giovanni

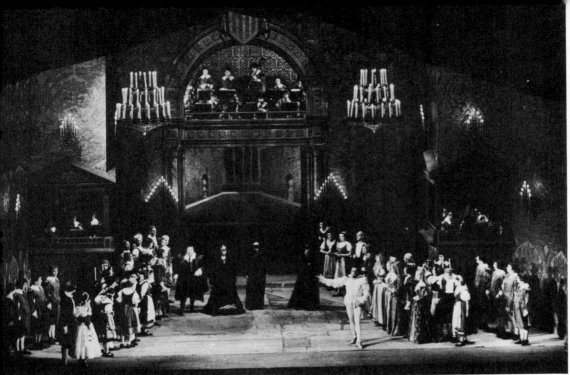

Donna Elvira and Donna Anna confront Don Giovanni at the wedding party of Masetto and Zerlina

Don Giovanni joins the peasants celebrating the wedding of Masetto and Zerlina

Leporello and Don Giovanni invite the statue of the Commendatore to supper

Donna Elvira (Eleanor Steber), Don Giovanni (Nicola Rossi-Lemeni), Don Ottavio (Cesare Valletti) and Donna Anna (Margaret Harshaw)

BY WOLFGANG AMADEUS MOZART
Libretto by Lorenzo da Ponte

In seventeenth century Seville the notorious and licentious Don Giovanni enters the apartments of Donna Anna at night. Her screams for help bring her father the Commendatore to the rescue, and in a brief sword fight the Commendatore is killed. Donna Anna has gone for help and returns with her fiance Ottavio to find her unknown assailant and his servant Leporello gone and her father dead. They swear vengeance upon the murderer.

At an inn Don Giovanni runs across a former sweetheart Elvira who is angry with him for leaving her. The Don departs leaving Leporello to tell the upset lady of his master's hundreds of affairs.

At a party peasants are celebrating the coming wedding of Masetto and Zerlina. Don Giovanni is fascinated by the girl and invites everyone to a ball at his palace, where he attempts to make love to Zerlina. The vengeful Elvira has followed and, meeting Ottavio and Donna Anna, the three of them prepare to keep watch at the ball, and confront the Don with his sins.

Despite these complications Don Giovanni continues his flirtations with Zerlina. When she cries for help from a room where the Don has taken her Ottavio, Zerlina, and Donna Anna rush to her rescue. Don Giovanni escapes, forcing a passage through the angry crowd with his sword.

In front of Elvira's house at night the Don pretends to repent and sings a song at her window. When Elvira comes out Leporello impersonates the Don and goes off with her leaving the Don free with Zerlina, Elvira's maid. When Zerlina's husband suddenly appears the Don quickly pretends to be Leporello and offers to help him catch the nobleman.

At night near a statue of the dead Commendatore Don Giovanni and Leporello are frightened to hear the statue speak to them. The defiant Don invites the statue to supper.

In the banquet hall the flickering lights go out as the ghostly figure appears to lead the cowering Don off into hell.

NOTES: WORLD PREMIERE: National Theatre, Prague, Bohemia, October 29, 1787. *Cast:* Donna Anna, Teresa Saporitti; Donna Elvira, Micelli; Zerlina, Bondini; Don Ottavio, Baglioni; Don Giovanni, Luigi Bassi; Leporello, Felice Ponziani. AMERICAN PREMIERE (in Italian): Park Theatre, New York, May 23, 1826. *Cast:* Zerlina, Maria Malibran; Don Giovanni, Manuel Garcia; Leporello, Manuel Garcia, Jr.; Donna Anna, Mme. Barbieri; Don Ottavio, Milon; Donna Elvira, Signora Garcia. An English version titled "The Libertine" was presented at Philadelphia, Pennsylvania, December 26, 1818. METROPOLITAN OPERA PREMIERE: November 28, 1883. *Cast:* Zerlina, Marcella Sembrich; Donna Anna, Emmy Fursch-Madi; Don Ottavio, Roberto Stagno; Don Giovanni, Giuseppe Kaschmann; Leporello, Giovanni Mirabella; Donna Elvira, Christine Nilsson.

Ezio Pinza as Don Giovanni.

Jarmila Novotna
as Donna Elvira

Leon Rothier
as the Commendatore

George London
as Don Giovanni

Dusolina Giannini
as Donna Anna

**Edouard De Reszke
as Leporello**

Victor Maurel sang Don Giovanni
at the Met for the first time, Dec. 31, 1894

**Geraldine Farrar
as Zerlina**

Nicola Rossi-Lemeni first sang Don Giovanni
at the Met Dec. 10, 1953

Bidu Sayao
as Zerlina

Tito Schipa
as Don Ottavio

Cesare Siepi
as Don Giovanni

Maurice Renaud
as Don Giovanni

Eugene Conley
as Don Ottavio

Antonio Scotti made his debut at the
Met, Dec. 27, 1899, in the role of Don
Giovanni. He last sang it April 3, 1908

Elisabeth Rethberg
as Donna Anna

Rose Bampton
as Donna Anna

Lucrezia Bori as Norina

Don Pasquale

MUSIC AND LIBRETTO
BY GAETANO DONIZETTI

An old bachelor Don Pasquale is angry at his nephew Ernesto for refusing to marry the woman picked out for him. The nephew loves an attractive widow, Norina. Don Pasquale's physician Dr. Malatesta suggests that the old man get married himself, and describes a very beautiful lady he claims is his sister. Pasquale is elated with this scheme and when Ernesto again refuses to give up the widow Don Pasquale says that he himself will marry and disinherit the young man. Desperately Ernesto begs his uncle to consult Dr. Malatesta before doing anything rash, but the Don gleefully tells him it was Dr. Malatesta himself who proposed the plan and offered his sister as bride. The news astonishes Ernesto who had thought the doctor was his friend.

Norina is reading a despairing note from Ernesto when Malatesta enters to tell her of his plan to make Don Pasquale agree to her marrying Ernesto. She must pretend to be his sister and go through a mock ceremony with Don Pasquale, then lead him a merry chase. She is persuaded this plan is her only hope of marrying Ernesto and she consents to play her part.

Papers are drawn up and Pasquale eagerly signs over to his bride half his property, much to Ernesto's distress. Once the papers are signed, Norina's attitude changes and she will not even permit Pasquale to kiss her. Instead she embarks on an expensive shopping tour taking Ernesto with her.

Evidences of the lavish buying spree are everywhere, and Don Pasquale is confronted with a mountain of bills. Pasquale learns of a tryst with Ernesto and he and Dr. Malatesta watch Norina's balcony at night where they surprise the two lovers. Dr. Malatesta reveals the plot and the false marriage and the old bachelor is so glad to get out of his costly alliance that he readily consents to a marriage between his nephew and the lovely but expensive Norina.

Vittorio Trevisan in title role

Salvatore Baccaloni as Don Pasquale with Bidu Sayao as Norina

Don Pasquale finally consents to his nephew's marriage to Norina

Bidu Sayao as Norina

Nino Martini as Ernesto

NOTES: WORLD PREMIERE: Theatre des Italiens, Paris, France, January 4, 1843. *Cast:* Norina, Giulia Grisi; Malatesta, Tamburini; Don Pasquale, Luigi Lablache; Ernesto, Giuseppe Mario. AMERICAN PREMIERE (in English): Park Theatre, New York, March 9, 1846. *Cast:* Don Pasquale, Arthur Edward Seguin; Norina, Mrs. Arthur Edward Seguin (Anne Childe); Malatesta, F. Mayer; Ernesto, Mr. Frazer. METROPOLITAN OPERA PREMIERE: January 8, 1900. *Cast:* Norina, Marcella Sembrich; Malatesta, Antonio Scotti; Don Pasquale, Antonio Pini-Corsi; Ernesto, Thomas Salignac.

Elektra

BY RICHARD STRAUSS
Libretto by Hugo Von Hofmannsthal

Queen Klytemnestra and her lover Aegisthus have murdered King Agamemnon. Not wanting her son Orestes around she had exiled him while still a young boy. Her daughters Elektra and Chrysothemis she humiliates shamefully, using them as servants and menials. The other servants deplore the wretched state of Elektra, but she is thinking only of her noble father's savage murder and of revenge. Chrysothemis warns her sister that Klytemnestra and Aegisthus plan to throw Elektra into jail, and though her gentle sister says it is better to die than live wretchedly, Elektra is defiant. When the queen enters her daughter hides her bitterness in soft words. The queen is restless and unhappy; she cannot sleep at night and suffers terrible dreams, and now seeks a cure. Elektra tells her there is one cure, the spilling of a woman's blood. When the queen demands to know what woman, her daughter is evasive, but predicts the deed will be done by a stranger, yet not a stranger, one of their own house. Thus she boldly predicts the death of her mother at Orestes' hands. The queen departs in terror.

An old man and a youth arrive at the palace telling of the death of Orestes, but Elektra refuses to believe the tidings. She denounces the youth for not protecting the life of her brother with his own, but soon learns that the youth is none other than Orestes himself. Wild with joy and passion at seeing him, she recounts the murder of her father and how the crime has obsessed her. Orestes is eager to avenge the wrong and the two of them await the final moment. Orestes enters the palace and there is a wild scream from the queen, murdered at the hands of her son. Aegisthus is led, with mock courtesy, to his doom by Elektra, and is in turn slain by Orestes. In a wild frenzy of joy Elektra dances until she falls senseless. The evil murders are avenged.

Rose Pauly as Elektra

**Elektra seeks vengeance
on her mother and step-father**

Friedrich Schorr as Orestes, Rose Pauly as Elektra

Astrid Varnay as Elektra

Jeanne Gerville-Reache as Klytemnestra

Gertrude Kappel, first Met Elektra

NOTES: WORLD PREMIÈRE: Dresden Hofoper. January 25, 1909. *Cast:* Elektra, Annie Krull; Klytemnestra, Ernestine Schumann-Heink; Chrysothemis, Margarete Siems; Aegisthus, Johannes Sembach; Orestes, Karl Perron. AMERICAN PREMIÈRE: Manhattan Opera House, New York City, February 1, 1910. *Cast:* Elektra, Mariette Mazarin; Klytemnestra, Jeanne Gerville-Reache; Chrysothemis, Alice Baron; Aegisthus, Duffault; Orestes, Gustav Huberdeau. METROPOLITAN OPERA PREMIÈRE: December 3, 1932. *Cast:* Elektra, Gertrude Kappel; Klytemnestra, Karin Branzell; Chrysothemis, Gota Ljungberg; Aegistheus, Rudolf Laubenthal; Orestes, Friedrich Schorr.

e Baron, American Chrysothemis

Gustav Huberdeau, first Orestes in America

Mariette Mazarin, first American Elektra

Huberdeau and Mazarin

L'Elisir d'Amore

BY GAETANO DONIZETTI
Libretto by Felice Romani

In an Italian village a well-to-do girl named Adina flirts outrageously with a young farmer Nemorino, and Belcore, the recruiting sergeant from a nearby town. Nemorino is ardent but Belcore persistent, and Adina treats them both badly. Into the village square comes Dr. Dulcamara, a quack who offers for sale an elixir of love. It is really only wine, but the gullible Nemorino buys a bottle and promptly gets drunk. Adina is shocked and astonished at this behavior and pretends that she will marry Belcore. The disheartened Nemorino would like another bottle of the love-potion, but since he has no money left, he is forced to enlist in the army under Belcore in order to get an advance on his salary before he has the coin to pay for more wine. And now he is really drunk.

The peasants are celebrating at the wedding feast, but the fickle Adina declares that she is not quite prepared to sign a marriage contract with Belcore. Dr. Dulcamara has meanwhile grown enthusiastic over the pretty lady and puts in his bid, too. Nemorino's rich uncle has died, and unknown to the poor boy, has left him all his money. This fact invests him with magic qualities and the village girls flock around him. Unaware of the real cause, Nemorino thinks it is the elixir of love which has made him so attractive. Adina, feeling now that she really loves Nemorino, is even willing to pay off his debt to Belcore and buy his release from the army. Seeing his suit is hopeless, the sergeant agrees, and amid general rejoicing Adina and Nemorino become engaged. The happy peasants think the quack's love potion has done the trick, and flock around his carriage to buy liberally.

Frieda Hempel as Adina and Enrico Caruso as Nemorino

NOTES: WORLD PREMIERE: Teatro della Canobbiana, Milan, Italy, May 12, 1832. *Cast:* Adina, Sabina Heinefetter; Nemorino, Il Genero; Belcore, Debadie; Dulcamara, Frezzolini. AMERICAN PREMIERE (in English): Park Theatre, New York City, June 18, 1838. *Cast:* Adina, Cardori-Allan; Giannetta, Mrs. Hughes; Nemorino. John Jones; Belcore, Morley; Dulcamara, Placide. METROPOLITAN OPERA PREMIERE: January 23, 1904. *Cast:* Adina, Marcella Sembrich; Giannetta, Isabelle Bouton; Nemorino, Enrico Caruso; Belcore, Antonio Scotti; Dulcamara, Archangelo Rossi.

Dr. Dulcamara, a quack, sells an elixir of love

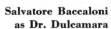

Salvatore Baccaloni as Dr. Dulcamara

Dulcamara's entrance

'Beniamino Gigli
as Nemorino

Ferruccio Tagliavini
as Nemorino

Elisabeth Rethberg
as Adina

Adina sings the Barcarolle with Dulcamara

Marcella Sembrich
as Adina

Adina and Nemorino rejoice at their engagement

Falstaff

BY GIUSEPPE VERDI
Libretto by Arrigo Boïto

The fat knight Falstaff is at the Garter Inn with Bardolph and Pistol where he writes two love letters, one for each of two highly respected ladies at Windsor, Mistress Page and Mistress Ford. When Bardolph and Pistol refuse to deliver the notes Falstaff kicks them out in a rage and has a boy take the letters.

In Ford's garden the two women compare their letters and decide, with the help of Bardolph, Pistol, and Ford, to have revenge. Dame Quickly is sent to invite the fat knight to an interview with Mistress Ford, and meanwhile the men plan to introduce Ford to Falstaff under an assumed name.

Back at the inn Bardolph and Pistol announce the arrival of Mistress Quickly with a note from Mistress Ford. The knight is to meet her that afternoon. In the meantime Falstaff has met Ford under the name Fortuna, who tells him he loves Mistress Ford and offers Falstaff money to intercede in his behalf. When Falstaff reveals he has a tryst with her that very afternoon Ford becomes honestly jealous.

Back in Ford's house Falstaff is just making love to Mistress Ford when he is interrupted by the arrival of Mistress Page. In a few moments the jealous and angry Ford arrives and the ladies hide the knight in a large clothes basket. To save Falstaff from Ford's jealousy the basket is ordered dumped in the river Thames.

A sad and stiff Falstaff receives Mistress Quickly later at the inn, and another meeting with Mistress Ford is arranged for that night in Windsor Forest.

In the dark as Falstaff begins his awkward love-making ghostly sounds interrupt him. The whole company enter in various disguises and give the frightened knight a thrashing. Satisfied with their sport, the revelers are unmasked and all ends happily.

NOTES: WORLD PREMIERE: La Scala, Milan. Italy, February 9, 1893. *Cast:* Mistress Ford, Emma Zilli; Mistress Page, Virginia Guerrini; Mistress Quickly, Giuseppini Pasqua; Ford, Antonio Pini-Corsi; Falstaff, Victor Maurel. AMERICAN PREMIERE: Metropolitan Opera House, New York City, February 4, 1895. *Cast:* Mistress Ford, Emma Eames; Mistress Page, Jane de Vigne; Mistress Quickly, Sofia Scalchi; Ford, Giuseppe Campanari; Falstaff, Victor Maurel.

Giacomo Rimini as Falstaff

Giuseppe Valdengo as Ford

Maria Gay, Mary Ranzenberg, Emmy Destinn and Frances Alda

Alessio De Paolis as Bardolph and
Lorenzo Alvary as Pistol

Victor Maurel as Falstaff

Norman Cordon as Pistol, Lawrence Tibbett as Falstaff
and Alessio De Paolis as Bardolph

Antonio Scotti as Falstaff

Falstaff makes love to Mistress Ford

Lawrence Tibbett as Ford

Falstaff reforms at last, declares life a joke

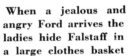

When a jealous and angry Ford arrives the ladies hide Falstaff in a large clothes basket

Queena Mario as Mistress Page

Victor Maur

Faust

BY CHARLES GOUNOD
**Libretto by Jules Barbier
and Michel Carré**

Mephistopheles, the devil, appears and shows the vision of a beautiful young girl to Faust, an aged philosopher, and offers him his youth in exchange for his soul.

The aged philosopher Faust despairs of solving life's secrets and prepares to take his own life. Suddenly the devil Mephistopheles appears to him, showing him a vision of a beautiful young girl, and promising to make Faust young again if he will relinquish his soul. Faust agrees and is miraculously transformed into an impetuous youth.

At the Kermess a festival is in progress. Valentin, about to go off to war, is worried at the prospect of leaving his sister Marguerite alone. Mephistopheles and Faust mingle with the crowd and the devil begins to tell fortunes. A mention of Marguerite's name enrages Valentin who rushes at Mephistopheles with drawn sword, but the evil one has drawn a magic circle around himself and cannot be harmed. Sensing the true identity of the stranger Valentin holds his sword like a cross and the fiend cowers before the sign. But soon everybody is dancing again and when Marguerite enters Faust offers her his arm.

In Marguerite's garden the devil tempts her with a basket of jewels, and while she adorns herself Faust watches unseen. Revealing himself he pleads passionately and wins her heart. They go off into the house leaving Mephistopheles gloating behind.

In the city street the soldiers are returning from war. Valentin learns Marguerite has been betrayed and, desperately attacking Faust, is mortally wounded. He dies cursing his sister.

Marguerite, driven insane by remorse for killing her child, seeks forgiveness in the church.

In a scene of wild revelry Mephistopheles shows Faust the horrors of hell, including a vision of Marguerite in chains. Faust insists on being taken instantly to the prison cell where she lies condemned to death for her crime. Faust realizes the consequences of his sin and urges her to escape with him, but her mind is broken. As Mephistopheles drags Faust off to Hell angels descend to lift Marguerite to heaven.

uard de Reszke as
phistopheles.

Valentin apostrophizes his sister
Marguerite's medal at the Kermess.

NOTES: WORLD PREMIERE: Theatre Lyrique, Paris, France, March 19, 1859. *Cast:* Marguerite, Caroline Marie Miolan-Carvalho; Faust, Joseph T. Barbot; Valentin, M. Regnal; Mephistopheles, M. Balanque. AMERICAN PREMIERE (in Italian): Academy of Music, New York City, November 25, 1863. *Cast:* Margherita, Clara Louise Kellogg; Faust, Francesco Mazzoleni; Mephistopheles, Hanibal Biachi; Valentin, G. Yppolito. METROPOLITAN OPERA PREMIERE (in Italian): October 22, 1883. *Cast:* Marguerite, Christine Nilsson; Faust, Italo Campanini; Mephistopheles, Franco Novara; Valentin, Giuseppe Del Puente. It is reputed to have been sung in German in Philadelphia, Pennsylvania, November 18, 1863, by a German company.

Mephistopheles (Nicola Rossi-Lemeni) mingles with the crowd during a festival at the Kermess. Scene from the Metropolitan Opera Company modernized production, premiered November 16, 1953.

Feodor Chaliapin as Mephistopheles, one of his most important roles. He sang the role in "Faust" in America for the first time at the Metropolitan Opera House January 6, 1908.

Faust watches Marguerite in her garden, while Mephistopheles woos old Marthe.

Riccardo Martin as Faust.

Leonard Warren as Valentin.

Adelina Patti as Marguerite.

Luisa Tetrazzini as Marguerite.

Queena Mario as Marguerite.

Enrico Caruso
as Faust.

Program of the
opening night of
the Metropolitan
Opera House.

Leon Rothier as
Mephistopheles.

Richard Bonelli
as Valentin.

The townsfolk
gather in church.

Charles Dalmores as Faust.

Frederick Jagel
as Faust.

Gladys Swarthout
as Siebel.

Lucien Muratore as Faust.

Ezio Pinza as Mephistopheles.

Christine Nilsson who made her debut as Marguerite
at the Metropolitan Opera House on its opening night,
October 22, 1883.

Emma Eames as Marguerite which
she first sang at the
Metropolitan Opera House,
December 25, 1891.

Marcel Journet
who appeared
as Mephistopheles
at the
Metropolitan
Opera House for
the first time on
December 28,
1901.

Vittorio Arimondi
as Mephistopheles.

Charles Hackett
as Faust.

Pol Plançon as Mephistopheles.

Geraldine Farrar as Marguerite and Giovanni Martinelli
as Faust.

Max Alvary as Faust which he sang
for the first time at the
Metropolitan Opera House
January 30, 1886.

Mary Garden as Marguerite.

Emma Calvé who
sang Marguerite
at the
Metropolitan
Opera House for
the first time
January 4, 1897.

Nellie Melba as Marguerite, one of
her most famous roles.

Minnie Hauk as Marguerite

Geraldine Farrar
as Marguerite

Amadeo Bassi as Faust   Thomas Chalmers as Valentin   Licia Albanese as Marguerite   Lawrence Tibbett as Valentin

Etelka Gerster as Marguerite

Frances Alda as Marguerite

Giannina Russ as Marguerite

Giuseppe Di Stefano as Faust

Felice Lyne as Marguerite

Grace Moore as Marguerite

Amanda Fabris as Marguerite

Cesare Siepi as Mephistopheles

Emma Juch as Marguerite

Marzelline has fallen in love with Leonore, disguised as the boy Fidelio

Margarete Matzenauer as Leonore

Fernando arrives to release Florestan from prison

Marianne Brandt, the first Met Fidelio. Her debut, November 19, 1884

Lotte Lehmann as Leonore

Fidelio

BY LUDWIG VAN BEETHOVEN
Libretto by Josef Sonnleithner

Hated by Don Pizarro, the governor of the prison, Florestan is thrown into jail purely from personal vengeance to die of starvation, thus making a violent murder unnecessary. In order to carry out his scheme Pizarro circulates the report that Florestan is dead, but his faithful wife Leonore cannot believe it. She disguises herself as a boy Fidelio and hires out to Rocco, the jailer, where she soon learns her husband is not yet dead but soon will be of starvation.

Meanwhile the jailer's daughter Marzelline falls in love with the 'youth' Fidelio. The selfless woman agrees to marry Marzelline, thus being sure to remain near her husband. The Minister of State Don Fernando is coming to inspect the prison, and Pizarro fears he may discover the unfortunate Florestan. He resolves to have the prisoner murdered at once. Rocco refuses to commit the act but agrees to dig the grave. Fidelio overhears the wicked scheme, and desperately wangles permission for all the prisoners to come out into the court for fresh air. She hopes to get a message to her husband, but he fails to appear with the others. In despair she goes with Rocco to help dig the grave.

In Florestan's dungeon the prisoner fails to recognize his wife but accepts bread from her. Pizarro enters to kill Florestan himself, but is prevented by Fidelio who holds him at pistol point. Trumpets announce the arrival of The Minister of State Fernando, and Florestan is saved.

In the courtyard Fernando congratulates Florestan on his escape and praises his faithful wife. The chains so lately on Florestan are now placed on Pizarro and he is led away to the darkness. Marzelline is comforted in her loss by finding another and real boy, the son of the gatekeeper.

NOTES: WORLD PREMIERE: Imperial and Royal Theatre an der Wien, Vienna, Austria, November 20, 1805. *Cast:* Don Fernando, Weinkoff; Don Pizarro, Meier; Florestan, Demmer; Leonore, Milder; Jaquino, Cache. AMERICAN PREMIERE (in English): Park Theatre, New York City, September 9, 1839. *Cast:* Don Fernando, Nickinson; Pizarro, Giubilei; Florestan, C. Manvers; Leonore, Mrs. Martyn; Jaquino, Edwin. METROPOLITAN OPERA PREMIERE: November 19, 1884. *Cast:* Don Fernando, Josef Staudigl; Don Pizarro, Adolf Robinson; Florestan, Anton Schott; Leonore, Marianne Brandt; Jaquino, Otto Kemlitz.

Kirsten Flagstad as Leonore

Die Fledermaus

BY JOHANN STRAUSS
Libretto by C. Haffner and Richard Genee

In nineteenth century Austria there is a Dr. Falke who seeks revenge on his rich friend Eisenstein, a prosperous Viennese, who has played a practical joke on him. Young Alfred is deeply in love with Rosalinda, Eisenstein's beautiful wife, and comes serenading her outside the window. Rosalinda's maid Adele appears with an invitation to a masked ball, but her mistress will not let her off for the evening. Meanwhile Eisenstein is faced with fourteen days in jail for offending an official, but Dr. Falke insists that he must postpone his imprisonment long enough to be able to attend a masked ball, and thus have an evening on the town away from his wife. After Eisenstein departs, presumably to spend the night in jail, Rosalinda hurries to welcome young Alfred. Together they sit down to enjoy an intimate supper; but are interrupted by the jailer who mistakes Alfred for Eisenstein. Rosalinda, suspecting her husband, persuades Alfred to take her husband's place in the jail for the night, while she determines to attend the ball in disguise.

Prince Orlofsky's brilliant ball is in progress and among the guests is Adele, dressed in Rosalinda's finery. She is recognized by the disguised Eisenstein, but laughs it off. Meanwhile Rosalinda enters in her disguise and soon captivates her unsuspecting husband. She manages to steal his watch. With wine, fine dancing, and music, the excitement of the ball rises to a climax.

The next day, Rosalinda hurries to the jail to release Alfred, and also to begin suit for divorce against her philandering husband. Meanwhile Eisenstein has returned to begin his sentence. When he finds his cell already occupied he learns from Alfred of his affair with his wife, Rosalinda. But his own anger dissipates when Rosalinda comes in flourishing the watch which she took from him at the ball. Both are equally guilty. Laughing over their escapades and embracing happily, Eisenstein and Rosalinda are reunited and the happy confusion is over.

NOTES: WORLD PREMIERE: Theater an der Wien, Vienna, Austria, April 5, 1874. *Cast:* Rosalinda, Marie Geistinger; Eisenstein, Szika; Adele, Mme. Charles Hirsch; Orlofsky, Nittinger; Alfred, Rudinger; Falke, Lebrecht. AMERICAN PREMIERE: Thalia Theatre, New York City, October 18, 1879. *Cast:* Rosalinda, Mathilde Cotrelly; Eisenstein, Max Schnelle; Adele, Emma Fiebach; Alfred, Lenoir; Orlofsky, Ahl; Falke, Fritze; Frank, Max Lube. METROPOLITAN OPERA PREMIERE: February 16, 1905. *Cast:* Rosalinda, Marcella Sembrich; Eisenstein, Andreas Dippel; Adele, Bella Alten; Alfred, Albert Reiss; Orlofsky, Edith Walker; Falke, Emil Greder; Frank, Otto Goritz.

Rosalinda welcomes
Alfred

Rosalinda finds her
husband Eisenstein and
Alfred both in jail

John Brownlee as Dr. Falke

Jarmila Novotna as Prince Orlofsky

Risë Stevens as Prince Orlofsky

Brenda Lewis as Rosalinda

Patrice Munsel as Adele

Mathilde Cotrelly,
first U. S. Rosalinda

Marcella Sembrich,
first Met Rosalinda

Senta muses about the legend of The Flying Dutchman

The Flying Dutchman

MUSIC AND LIBRETTO BY RICHARD WAGNER

A wild storm drives a sea captain named Daland into a small bay off the coast of Norway. He goes ashore to find he is near home but the storm prevents going further. The captain has returned to his ship and anchored for the night when 'The Flying Dutchman,' a legendary phantom ship with blood red sails and black masts, slips in and silently drops anchor. The ghostly captain of the phantom ship is permitted to go ashore once every seven years. If he finds a woman who will remain faithful to him the awful curse will be lifted. Another seven years is over and the strange captain asks for shelter with Daland. Learning the Norwegian has a daughter the Dutchman proposes marriage and offers a large sum of gold. Daland agrees to the proposal.

Daland's daughter Senta muses at her spinning wheel about the familiar legend of the Flying Dutchman. She longs to meet him and by her fidelity lift the curse. Daland arrives with the Dutchman and Senta is soon in love with him. She pledges her fidelity to death and the exultant Dutchman believes his hour of freedom has come.

In the harbor the Norwegian ship is lighted for a celebration while next to her is the dark shape of the ghost ship. Weird lights glow from the strange ship and the sailors are troubled. Senta is begged not to follow the Dutchman, and coming on her suddenly he believes she has been false to him and that all is lost. Aboard the Phantom ship the red sails swell and it moves slowly out of the harbor to sea. Faithful to death, Senta throws her-self into the sea from a cliff, crying 'I am faithful unto death.' The phantom ship sinks, but Senta and the strange captain are united in death and the curse is lifted.

NOTES: WORLD PREMIERE: Royal Opera House, Dresden, Germany, January 2, 1843. *Cast:* Daland, Karl Risse; Senta, Wilhemine Schroeder-Devrient; Erik, Reinhold; Mary, Mme. J. M. Wachter; Dutchman, Johann Michael Wachter. AMERICAN PREMIERE (in Italian): Academy of Music, Philadelphia, Pa., by the Pappenheim Opera Company. *Cast:* Daland, T. J. Sullivan; Mary, Mlle. Cooney; Dutchman, Felix Preusser; Senta, Eugenia Pappenheim; Erik, Pietro Baccei. METROPOLITAN OPERA PREMIERE (in German): November 27, 1889. *Cast:* Daland, Emil Fischer; Senta, Sophie Wiesner; Erik, Paul Kalisch; Mary, Charlotte Huhn; Dutchman, Theodore Reichmann.

Kirsten Flagstad sang her first Senta January 7, 1937

Senta sings her Ballad

The Norwegian ship is lighted for a celebration

Eleanor Steber made
her opera debut as
Senta, 1936, in Boston
at the Opera House

Schumann-Heink as Mary

Emmy Destinn as Senta

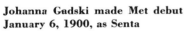
Johanna Gadski made Met debut
January 6, 1900, as Senta

Herbert Janssen in title role

Friedrich Schorr
as the Dutchman

La Forza del Destino

(The Force of Destiny)

BY GIUSEPPE VERDI
Libretto by Francesco Maria Piave

Don Alvaro has fallen in love with Leonora, the daughter of the Marquis of Calatrava, and though her father strongly opposes the marriage she determines to elope. The elopement is interrupted by the Marquis who is accidentally killed by Alvaro. He dies cursing his horror-stricken daughter.

At an inn near Hornacuelos Don Carlo, the son of the dead Marquis, disguised as a student, seeks to avenge his father's death. Leonora is terrified to find her brother has sworn to kill Alvaro and herself, and flees to a nearby convent.

The unhappy woman confesses to an abbot and is admitted to the Convent of Hornacuelos. Dressed as a nun, she is directed to a cave nearby where she will be safe. The abbot promises to curse anyone who seeks to find her there.

Meanwhile Alvaro, praying for forgiveness, has fled to Italy and joined the army. In battle he saves the life of Don Carlo, who has gone searching for him. Not knowing the identity of each other they swear eternal friendship. Alvaro is shortly afterward seriously wounded and believing himself dying entrusts Carlo with a packet of letters which must be destroyed. Alvaro does not die and his identity becomes known to Don Carlo. In a fight Alvaro believes he has killed Don Carlo and resolves to end his life in a monastery.

Years later at the inn near Hornacuelos Alvaro is once again discovered by the vengeful Don Carlo and the feud is reopened.

On a wild spot near a cave the two men fight and Don Carlo is mortally wounded. Leonora emerges from the cave to embrace her dying brother, but true to his vow he stabs her through the heart. Don Alvaro throws himself from a cliff as monks from the monastery arrive singing the miserere.

NOTES: WORLD PREMIERE: Imperial Italian Theatre, St. Petersburg, Russia, November 10, 1862. *Cast:* Donna Leonora, Mme. Barbot; Don Alvaro, Enrico Tamberlik; Don Carlo, Francesco Graziani; Fra Melitone, Alberto de Bassini. AMERICAN PREMIERE: Academy of Music, New York City, February 24, 1865. *Cast:* Donna Leonora, Carlotta Carozzi-Zucchi; Don Alvaro, Bernardo Massimiliani; Fra Melitone, Dubreuil. METROPOLITAN OPERA PREMIERE: November 15, 1918. *Cast:* Marquis, Louis D'Angelo; Donna Leonora, Rosa Ponselle (debut); Don Carlo, Giuseppe DeLuca; Don Alvaro, Enrico Caruso; Abbot, José Mardones; Melitone, Thomas Chalmers.

Enrico Caruso sang Don Alvaro at first Met performance Nov. 15, 1918

Leonora (Zinka Milanov)
begs her father's (Lubomir
Vichegonov) mercy for
her lover Don Alvaro
(Richard Tucker) as Curra
(Thelma Votipka) watches

Peasants and soldiers celebrate
the victory over Austria
at Valletri

The friars pray for
divine protection for
the penitent
fugitive, Leonora

Scene from first Met production with
José Mardones, Enrico Caruso, Rosa Ponselle

**Richard Tucker
as Don Alvaro**

**Leonard Warren sang his first Met
performance of Don Carlos
Jan. 24, 1944**

**Frederick Jagel
as Don Alvaro**

**Zinka Milanov
as Leonora**

**Lawrence Tibbett
as Don Carlos**

Rosa Ponselle sang Leonora at her
Metropolitan debut November 15, 1918

Gianni Schicchi

BY GIACOMO PUCCINI
Libretto by Gioachino Forzano

In Tuscany during the thirteenth century the family of Rinuccio are greatly disturbed because one of their relatives, Signor Donati, has just passed away leaving his great wealth to the Church. They wish to consult the shrewd peasant, Gianni Schicchi, whose daughter Lauretta is in love with Rinuccio, in the hope that he may prove smart enough to find a way to invalidate Donati's will so that they can inherit his money. As Donati's death is not yet public knowledge, Schicchi schemes to impersonate the old Donati and dictate a new will, and thus leave the estate to Rinuccio's family. Into the dead man's bed climbs Gianni Schicchi, while a lawyer and notary are called to take down the new will. But after bequeathing a few unimportant baubles to the legitimate heirs he boldly leaves the bulk of the fortune to himself. The indignant relatives clustered around the bed protest among themselves against this treachery, but dare not expose the trick to the lawyers for fear of being punished for their part. After the lawyer and notary depart the relatives attack Schicchi, but he seizes a cane and beats them off. Cursing heartily, the duped relatives depart. Lauretta and Rinuccio, eventual heirs to the money, are united by the clever Gianni Schicchi.

Nino Martini as Rinuccio

Giuseppe Di Stefano as Rinuccio

Nadine Conner as Lauretta

Italo Tajo as Gianni Schicchi

Kathleen Howard as Zita   Giulio Crimi as Rinuccio   Florence Easton as Lauretta   Giuseppe De Luca as Gianni Schicchi

Gianni Schicchi dictates the will

NOTES: WORLD PREMIERE: Metropolitan Opera House, New York, New York, December 14, 1918. *Cast:* Gianni Schicchi, Giuseppe DeLuca; Lauretta, Florence Easton; Zita, Kathleen Howard; Rinuccio, Giulio Crimi; Nella, Marie Tiffany; Nicolao, Andreas de Segurola.

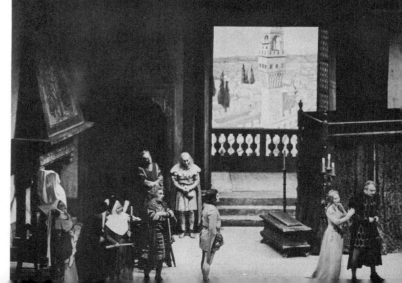

Lauretta pleads for Rinuccio

[97]

La Gioconda

BY AMILCARE PONCHIELLI
Libretto by Arrigo Boïto

Venice, the Seventeenth Century. The ballad singer La Gioconda is stopped in the ducal square as she leads her blind mother by Barnaba, a spy for the Inquisition. She is in love with Enzo and spurns his attentions. Barnaba is enraged and attempts to stir up the people against Gioconda's mother, claiming she is a witch. The mob is prevented from harming her by the appearance of Alvise, a leader of the Inquisition, and his wife Laura. Barnaba notices the passionate looks between Laura and Enzo and manages to whisper to Enzo that Laura intends to visit him that night on his ship. To Laura's husband he tells the same story. Gioconda overhears, heartbroken at the faithlessness of Enzo.

On board Enzo's vessel the two lovers meet and plan to sail away at dawn, but Gioconda enters to denounce Laura. Laura's husband Alvise approaches and Gioconda generously helps Laura escape. Rather than have his ship captured by Barnaba, Enzo sets it afire.

In the palace of Alvise, the Inquisitor declares Laura must die and orders her to drink poison. Gioconda substitutes a harmless narcotic for the poison and Laura falls into a deathlike trance.

At a grand ball Barnaba whispers to Enzo that Laura is dead by Alvise's hand. In the confusion that follows Enzo denounces the Inquisitor and is in turn arrested, with Barnaba as his guard. Gioconda agrees to give herself to the spy if he will release Enzo.

To a ruined palace on the Adriatic, Gioconda has brought the unconscious Laura, who is revived when Enzo appears. As the lovers escape and Barnaba comes to claim his reward, Gioconda stabs herself. But Barnaba has his last revenge, as he shouts to the dying woman that he has murdered her blind mother.

Enzo meets Laura near his boat

NOTES: WORLD PREMIERE: La Scala, Milan, Italy, April 8, 1876. *Cast:* La Gioconda, Mariani; Laura, Biancolini; La Cieca, Barlandini; Enzo, Gayapro; Barnaba, Aldighieri. American Premiere: Metropolitan Opera House, New York City, December 20, 1883. *Cast:* Laura, Emmy Fursch-Madi; La Cieca, Sofia Scalchi; Enzo, Roberto Stagno; Barnaba, Giuseppe del Puente; La Gioconda, Christine Nilsson.

The guests gather in the palace of Alvise for a grand ball

Gioconda gives her blessing to the two lovers,
Enzo and Laura, before killing herself

Lillian Nordica
as Gioconda

Riccardo Martin as Enzo

Rosa Ponselle
as Gioconda

Beniamino Gigli as Enzo

Mario Ancona as Barnaba

Maurice Renaud
as Enzo

Eleanor De Cisneros
as Gioconda

Zinka Milanov as Gioconda

Giacomo Lauri-Volpi
as Enzo

Enrico Caruso as Enzo

Fedora Barbieri as Laura

Pasquale Amato as Barnaba

Louise Homer
as Laura

Gotterdammerung

Siegfried swears fealty to Gunther on Hagen's spear

MUSIC AND LIBRETTO BY RICHARD WAGNER

Leaving Brunnhilde in search of new adventures Siegfried gives her as a pledge of his love the Ring of the Nibelung, which carries an everlasting curse with it.

He descends the Rhine Valley to the Hall of King Gunther who lives with his sister Gutrune and his half-brother Hagen, who knows the history of the ring and desires to bring it back to his father. Gunther desires to woo Brunnhilde; thus, after Siegfried is warmly greeted he is given a secret drink which makes him forget Brunnhilde and fall in love with Gutrune. The king agrees to let Gutrune marry Siegfried if he, Gunther, can win Brunnhilde. In order to help him Siegfried assumes the shape of Gunther and starts back to Brunnhilde.

The goddess is startled to find a stranger penetrating the magic circle of fire around her rock which none but Siegfried may cross. Siegfried takes the ring from her finger and draws her into the cave.

On the bank of the Rhine Hagen and Alberich plan to win back the ring. Siegfried returns, announcing he has won Brunnhilde for Gunther. At the wedding feast Brunnhilde is grief-stricken at the sight of Siegfried, now in his own appearance, making love to Gutrune. She sees the ring on her hero's finger and demands an explanation. Siegfried, still having no memory of Brunnhilde, cannot reply. Hagen promises to avenge Brunnhilde and she tells him Siegfried is only vulnerable in the back. They plot to slay Siegfried for treachery.

In the forest the Rhine Maidens beg Siegfried to return the ring. He refuses, and the maidens declare he will die that day. Horns announce Gunther and Hagen. At the opportune moment Hagen plunges his spear into Siegfried's back. The body is borne into the hall and Hagen demands the ring. Gunther refuses to give it up and a battle follows. Hagen kills Gunther, but when he attempts to take the ring from the dead man's finger Siegfried's arm rises menacingly. Brunnhilde orders a funeral pyre on the bank of the Rhine and, mounting her horse, rides into the flames. The Rhine Maidens snatch the ring from the fire. Valhalla burns, and the gods await their doom.

NOTES: WORLD PREMIERE: Bayreuth Festival Theatre, August 17, 1876. *Cast:* Siegfried, George Unger; Gunther, Eugene Gura; Hagen, Gustav Siehr; Alberich, Karl Hill; Gutrune, Mathilde Weckerlin; 1st Norn, Johanna Jachmann-Wagner; 2nd Norn, Josephine Scheffsky; 3rd Norn, Fredericke Sadler Grun; Woglinde, Lilli Lehmann; Wellgunde, Marie Lehmann; Flosshilde, Minna Lammert; Brunnhilde, Amalia Materna. AMERICAN PREMIERE: Metropolitan Opera House, New York City, January 25, 1888. *Cast:* Siegfried, Albert Niemann; Gunther, Adolf Robinson; Hagen, Emil Fischer; Alberich, Rudolph von Milde; Brunnhilde, Lilli Lehmann; Gutrune, Auguste Seidl-Kraus; Woglinde, Sophie Traubmann; Wellgunde, Marianne Brandt; Flosshilde, Louise Meisslinger. The Norn and Waltraute scenes were not given in this production.

Ludwig Hofmann as Hagen

A Met rehearsal of Siegfried's arrival at Gunther's Hall.
Note absence of wigs

Jean de Reszke
as Siegfried

Milka Ternina
as Brunnhilde

Regina Resnik
as Gutrune

Ernestine Schumann-Heink
as Waltraute

Edouard de Reszke
as Hagen

[103]

Helen Traubel as Brunnhilde

Alexander Kipnis as Hagen

Kathleen Howard as Waltraute

Margaret Harshaw as Waltraute

Lilli Lehmann as Brunnhilde

Lilian Nordica
as Brunnhilde

The Witch's spell is broken

Hansel und Gretel

BY ENGELBERT HUMPERDINCK
Libretto by Adelheid Wette

Two hungry children, Hansel and Gretel, try to forget their misery by dancing and singing as they work. When their mother returns to find them neglecting their tasks she scolds them and sends them off to pick strawberries in the woods. Meanwhile their father returns from the village where he has had a successful day selling his brooms. He has brought a big basketful of food. When his wife tells him the children have gone off into the woods looking for strawberries he is alarmed. Deep in the woods lives a wicked witch who lures children with magic things to eat. The upset mother and father hurry out to look for their children.

Night is falling in the deep woods where Hansel and Gretel have been picking berries. Afraid and in the dark, the children lose their way, and their fear increases as they imagine all sorts of monsters peering out at them. A sandman comes to put them to sleep after they have said their prayers. From out of the mists a ladder appears and fourteen angels descend to watch over the children while they sleep.

In the morning the children awaken to tell each other their dreams. The mists rise revealing the witch's magic little house all made of candy and surrounded by a gingerbread fence. The children are hungry and begin to nibble at the fence when suddenly the witch rushes out, captures Hansel, and spirits him into a cage. Gretel is made to fetch almonds and raisins to fatten Hansel so that he may be baked into gingerbread. The wicked witch fires up the oven and asks Gretel to look inside to see if it is hot enough. Gretel pretends to be clumsy and asks to see how it is done. When the witch bends over to show her Gretel and Hansel, who has escaped, push her in and shut the door. All the children who have been turned into gingerbread now come back to life. Hansel and Gretel are found by their parents and all ends happily.

NOTES: WORLD PREMIERE: Weimar, Germany, December 23, 1893. *Cast:* Hansel, Miss Schubert; Gretel, Miss Tebelli; Gertrude, Miss Kayster; Witch, Miss Fink; Peter, Mr. Wiedey; Sandman, Miss Hartwick. AMERICAN PREMIERE (in English): Daly's Theatre, New York City, October 8, 1895. *Cast:* Peter, Jacques Bars; Gertrude, Alice Gordon; Witch, Louise Meisslinger; Hansel, Marie Elba; Gretel, Jeane Douste; Sandman, Cecile Brani; Dewman, Edith Johnston. METROPOLITAN OPERA PREMIERE: November 25, 1905; *Cast:* Hansel, Lina Abarbanell; Gretel, Bella Alten; Gertrude, Marion Weed; Witch, Louise Homer; Sandman, Florence Mulford; Dewman, Roberta Glanville; Peter, Otto Goritz.

Lina Abarbanell who sang Hansel at the Met premiere

Hansel and Gretel meet the wicked Witch

Queena Mario as Gretel, her most famous role

Angels descend to watch over the children

Bella Alten was the first to sing Gretel at the Met

Nadine Conner as Gretel

Herodiade

BY JULES MASSENET
Libretto by Miller and Gremont

Salome has come to the courtyard of Herod's palace searching for the Prophet John with whom she is infatuated. The Chaldean Phanuel is astonished to find Salome there and wonders if she knows that Queen Herodias is her mother. Salome declares that John, who saved her from the desert when she was a child, is a genuinely good and kind man. Herodias is enraged at the Prophet for calling her Jezebel and demands that Herod execute him. Herod hesitates, while the Prophet enters and denounces both King and Queen, who flee before his scorn. Salome confesses her love and tenderly the Prophet bids her turn to God.

Herod longs to possess his wife's daughter and, taking a mysterious drug, sees Salome's face in a vision. His sleep is interrupted by Phanuel who warns him the people are being stirred up by John and are ready to revolt.

In the public square Herod kneels before the Roman Proconsul Vitellius. Herodias denounces John to the Roman and warns of the Prophet's growing power. John courageously declares that all power comes from God.

Herodias seeks guidance from astrology. Only disaster is written in her horoscope, and she is horrified to find it is her daughter Salome who has usurped her place in Herod's affections.

In the temple Herod pleads for Salome's love, but she spurns him. John is brought before Herod, and though Salome begs for his life, is condemned to death.

In prison John prays to be free of Salome's love. When she comes to him they embrace tenderly, before soldiers lead John to execution.

At a great feast Salome begs Herod for John's life, but her pleading ends when soldiers enter with the Prophet's head. Desperately Salome attempts to kill Herodias, but the Queen reveals herself as Salome's mother. Horror-stricken, Salome takes her own life.

Lina Cavalieri as Salome

Cyrena Van Gordon as Herodias

NOTES: WORLD PREMIERE: Theatre de la Monnaie, Brussels, Belgium, December 19, 1881. AMERICAN PREMIERE: French Opera House, New Orleans, La., February 13, 1892. NEW YORK PREMIERE: Manhattan Opera House, November 8, 1909. *Cast:* John, Charles Dalmores; Herod, Maurice Renaud; High Priest, Jean Vallier; Salome, Lina Cavalieri; Herodias, Jeanne Gerville-Réache; Phanuel, Vallier; Vitellius, Armand Crabbe.

Maurice Renaud as Herod

Emmy Destinn as Valentine in "Les Huguenots"

Les Huguenots

BY GIACOMO MEYERBEER
Libretto by Eugène Scribe
and Émile Deschamps

In France during the sixteenth century Marguerite de Valois attempts to reconcile the bitter religious strife between Catholics and Protestant Huguenots, which culminated in the Massacre of St. Bartholomew. In Count De Nevers' Palace the Catholics are surprised by the arrival of Raoul, a prominent Huguenot, who tells of his rescue that morning of a beautiful woman from some drunken revellers. Though he does not know her identity, she is Valentine, daughter of St. Bris, a leader of the Catholic party. A veiled woman comes to see Nevers, and Raoul, surprised to see it is the beautiful woman he rescued, concludes she is Nevers' mistress. But Valentine has fallen in love with Raoul and has come only to break her engagement to Nevers.

In the gardens of Marguerite, Valentine notifies the Queen that her engagement is broken. Raoul is brought before the Queen who wishes this outstanding Protestant to marry Valentine, of the Catholic faction, thus attempting to heal the religious breach. Raoul is astounded by the proposal, believing Valentine is Nevers' mistress, and refuses the engagement. St. Bris is enraged at the insult and feelings between the two parties are further inflamed.

Valentine, now married to Nevers, overhears Catholics plotting the murder of Raoul and attempts to warn him. The Queen prevents bloodshed, and Raoul, now realizing his injustice to Valentine, is remorseful.

Raoul secretly meets Valentine in Nevers' Palace, where they overhear St. Bris and other Catholics plot the St. Bartholomew massacre. Horrified, Raoul finds he is too late to warn the Huguenots.

During the massacre which follows Raoul is mortally wounded. Valentine finds him dying in the street. As she kneels at his side, St. Bris and the other Catholics fire on them, and the lovers perish together.

Enrico Caruso as Raoul

NOTES: WORLD PREMIERE: Paris Opera House, Paris, France, February 29, 1836. *Cast:* Valentine, Marie C. Falcon; Marguerite, Julia A. Dorus-Gras; Urbain, Mlle. Flecheux; Raoul, Adolphe Nourrit; Count de Nevers, M. Derivis. AMERICAN PREMIERE: Theatre d'Orleans, New Orleans, Louisiana, April 29, 1839. METROPOLITAN OPERA PREMIERE (in Italian): March 19, 1884. *Cast:* Valentine, Christine Nilsson; Marguerite, Marcella Sembrich; Urbain, Sofia Scalchi; Raoul, Italo Campanini; Count de Nevers, Giuseppe del Puente.

Giuseppe Del Puente sang Count de Nevers at the Met premiere

Italo Campanini as Raoul

Jean Lassalle as Count de Nevers

Antonio Scotti as Count de Nevers

Christine Nilsson sang Valentine at the Met premiere

Jean de Reszke as Raoul

Sofia Scalchi who sang Urbain
at the Met premiere

Pol Plancon
as Count de St. Bris

Mabel Garrison as Urbain

Rosa Ponselle as Rachel

Enrico Caruso as Eleazar, Rosa Ponselle as Rachel

La Juive

BY JACQUES HALÉVY
Libretto by Eugène Scribe

The time is 1414. In the square before the Cathedral all the townspeople of Constance celebrate the victories of Prince Leopold except the aged Jew Eleazar, who works at his shop. Enraged by this behavior the people arrest Eleazar and are about to lynch him when the Cardinal emerges from the Cathedral and silences the crowd. He recognizes Eleazar as a Jew he knew years previously in Rome, and in turn the Jew recognizes the churchman as an anti-Jewish fanatic who killed his two sons. In revenge, Eleazar had set fire to the Cardinal's house and stolen his daughter. This girl, Rachel, he has raised as his own child. The Cardinal is ready to forget old enmities but Eleazar refuses, swearing vengeance.

In Eleazar's shop Prince Leopold, disguised as a Jew, courts Rachel, though he is already engaged to the Princess Eudoxia. When the Princess enters the shop unexpectedly and Leopold quickly hides, Rachel is deeply troubled. Confessing he is not a Jew, Leopold begs Rachel to flee with him. Eleazar attempts to kill him when he discovers the deception, but is prevented by Rachel.

At the Palace Rachel sees Leopold with Eudoxia and, overcome with jealousy, accuses him of being her lover.

The Cardinal angrily excommunicates Leopold and demands a hideous death for the Jews.

The Cardinal urges Eleazar in prison to save himself by being converted. Refusing, Eleazar tells the churchman that he knows the whereabouts of his long lost daughter, but refuses to say where she is. The Cardinal sadly departs.

Eleazar confesses to Rachel her real parentage, but the devout girl prefers to die a Jewess than live a Christian. After she has been burned in boiling oil, Eleazar tells the Cardinal he has executed his own child. His vengeance complete, Eleazar joins Rachel in death.

NOTES: WORLD PREMIERE: Academie de Musique, Paris, France, February 23, 1835. *Cast:* Rachel, Cornelia Falcon; Eudoxia, Mme. Dorus-Gras; Eleazar, Adolphe Nourrit; Cardinal, Nicolas Levasseur. AMERICAN PREMIERE: Theatre d'Orleans, New Orleans, La., February 13, 1844. METROPOLITAN OPERA PREMIERE (in German): January 16, 1885. *Cast:* Rachel, Amalia Materna; Eleazar, Anton Udvardy; Leopold, Herr Schueller; Brogni, Josef Kugel; Princess, Marie Schroder-Hanfstangl. In Act 3, Mme. Schroder-Hanfstangl introduced the air of Isabell from Meyerbeer's opera "Robert Le Diable."

Enrico Caruso as Eleazar. His last appearance on any stage was in this role at the Met, December 24, 1920

Giovanni Martinelli as Eleazar

Elisabeth Rethberg as Rachel

A sacred garden in India

Giovanni Martinelli as Gerald with Maria Barrientos as Lakmé

Ezio Pinza as Nilakantha

Lakme

BY LÉO DELIBES
Libretto by Edmond Gondinet
and Philippe Gille

In a sacred garden in India Lakmé and her slave go into the jungle to gather flowers. During her absence some English visitors appear and are charmed by the beauty of the sacred place. One of them, Gerald, remains behind after the others depart in order to make sketches, in spite of the warnings of his friends. When Lakmé reappears the impressionable young people fall deeply in love. After he has finally departed, Lakmé's father Nilakantha, a Brahman priest comes to discover the garden has been defiled. He swears vengeance upon the intruder and only a thunderstorm prevents him from following Gerald and killing him at once.

In the market place Nilakantha and Lakmé are disguised as beggars. Hoping to attract the Englishman Nilakantha orders his daughter to sing a song while he accompanies her on the bells. Gerald is in the crowd and recognizes the voice. As he attempts to approach her he is stabbed by the vengeful father. Not believing him dead, Lakmé has his body carried away by her servants.

In a hut deep in the forest Lakmé nurses Gerald back to health. She goes out seeking magic water which according to Hindoo superstition will make him faithful to death if he drinks it. During her absence Gerald's friend Frederick finds him and begs him to return to his duty. When Lakmé returns Gerald gently tells her he desires to go back with Frederick. The anguished Lakmé poisons herself with the juice of a deadly flower and dies in his arms.

NOTES: WORLD PREMIERE: Opera Comique. Paris, France, April 14, 1883. *Cast:* Lakmé, Marie Van Zandt; Nilakantha, Cabolet; Frederick, Barre; Gerald, Talazac. FIRST ADEQUATE PRODUCTION IN THE UNITED STATES by the American Opera Company at the Academy of Music, New York City, March 1, 1886. *Cast:* Lakmé, Pauline L. Allemand; Nilakantha, Alonzo Stoddard; Frederick, W. H. Lee; Gerald, William Canddus. METROPOLITAN OPERA PREMIERE: February 22, 1892. *Cast:* Lakmé, Marie Van Zandt; Nilakantha, Edouard de Reszke; Frederick, Jean Martapoura; Gerald, Sebastian Montariol.

Lily Pons as Lakmé

Pauline L'Allemand, the first U. S. Lakmé

Luisa Tetrazzini as Lakmé

Leon Rothier as Nilakantha

Marie Van Zandt, creator of Lakmé

[116]

Giovanni Martinelli with Giuseppe
De Luca

Maria Barrientos as Lakmé

Amelita Galli-Curci
as Lakmé

Tito Schipa
as Gerald

The swan boat bearing Lohengrin appears in answer to Elsa's prayers

Lohengrin

MUSIC AND LIBRETTO BY RICHARD WAGNER

King Henry of Germany arrives in Brabant in the 10th century to find the state in anarchy. The son of the late duke has disappeared. The regent Telramund, incited by his wife Ortrud, claims the throne and insists the young heir was murdered by his sister Elsa. Faced with this charge Elsa declares her innocence and is willing to submit to the ordeal by combat. For her defender she calls for a knight she has seen only in her dreams. A strange knight appears in a boat drawn by a swan. He has come to defend Elsa but wishes to remain unknown. In combat he defeats Telramund but spares his life. He asks Elsa's hand in marriage and she accepts.

The night before the wedding Ortrud and Telramund appear in the courtyard. Ortrud urges Telramund to attempt to regain what has been lost. Calling to Elsa who appears on the balcony Ortrud begs to be forgiven.

At daybreak the wedding ceremonies begin. Ortrud appears magnificently dressed at the church door and accuses the knight of being a magician who unfairly gained a victory over Telramund. The knight refuses to reveal his identity, and as Elsa declares her confidence in him they enter the church.

After the bridal ceremony the couple are alone. Elsa is unable to forget Ortrud's insinuations and despite her vow asks the forbidden questions. Before he can answer Telramund rushes into the room to attack but is driven back and killed. Turning once more to Elsa the knight sorrowfully tells her that he will explain everything to the king.

The court gathers to hear the strange knight explain that he is Lohengrin, son of Parsifal and a knight of the Holy Grail and permitted to be absent on good deeds only as long as he remains unknown. Now he must return. Lohengrin bids farewell to Elsa as the boat with the swan reappears. Suddenly the swan changes into a young man, Elsa's brother who had been transformed by the magic of Ortrud. As Elsa sinks in her brother's arms Lohengrin disappears in the boat, now drawn by a dove.

NOTES: WORLD PREMIERE: Court Theatre, Weimar, Germany, August 28, 1850. *Cast:* Lohengrin, Carl Beck; Telramund, Theodor von Milde; King Henry, Hoefer; Elsa, Rosa von Milde Aegthe; Ortrud, Fastlinger. AMERICAN PREMIERE: Stadt Theatre, New York City, April 3, 1871. *Cast:* Lohengrin, Theodor Habelmann; Telramund, Vierling; King Henry, Franosch; Elsa, Louise Lichtmay; Ortrud, Frederici. METROPOLITAN OPERA PREMIERE (in Italian): November 7, 1883. *Cast:* Lohengrin, Italo Campanini; Telramund, Giuseppe Kaschman; King Henry, Franco Novara; Ortrud, Emmy Fursch-Madi; Elsa, Christine Nilsson. First Metropolitan Opera performance in German, November 23, 1885.

Lohengrin asks Elsa's faith

Telramund is slain by Lohengrin

Astrid Varnay
and Lauritz Melchior

Max Alvary as Lohengrin

Rose Bampton with Lauritz Melchior

Julia Claussen

Marianne Brandt

Rose Pauly

Famous Ortruds

Margarete Matzenauer

Margaret Harshaw

Cyrena Van Gordon

Italo Campanini,
first Met Lohengrin

Johannes Sembach as Lohengrin

Jean de Reszke, first
American appearance as
Lohengrin in Chicago,
November 9, 1891

Helen Traubel
as Elsa

Emma Eames as Els

Louise refuses to elope with Julien

The dressmaking girls make fun of Louise for being in love

Louise is to be the Queen of Montmartre

Louise

MUSIC AND LIBRETTO
BY GUSTAVE CHARPENTIER

Paris in the spring, and in a tenement Louise cannot keep her mind on her work while her lover, the artist Julien, is across the alley. Louise's mother despises the artist for his shiftlessness, but her father is more lenient and sensible on the subject. After the mother and daughter quarrel violently the father attempts to reason kindly with Louise and she regretfully promises to try to forget Julien.

In the early morning in Montmartre strange characters appear, scavengers, rag-pickers, laborers. Julien waits with friends for Louise to pass on her way to work in a dressmaker's shop. He wants her to elope with him but she refuses.

Inside the shop the girls sing while they work, and make fun of Louise for being in love. Julien's voice is heard outside and Louise, pretending to be sick, hurries out to join him.

Julien and Louise live together happily for a time in Montmartre. It is a time of celebrations and Louise is to be the Queen of Montmartre. In the midst of the bohemian gayety Louise's mother appears with news that her father is near death. The distracted mother begs Julien to release Louise and reluctantly he does so, after she promises to return.

Once back home Louise discovers she has been tricked and is held virtually a prisoner. Her father attempts once more to reason with the sullen and rebellious girl but the urge to return to Julien and her carefree life is too strong. Finally, in a fit of anger she is ordered out of the house. She hurries down the stairs and into the streets as her unhappy father calls her name from the window. But Louise is gone forever, another victim swallowed up by the city.

NOTES: WORLD PREMIERE: Opéra Comique, Paris, France, February 2, 1900. *Cast:* Louise, Marthe Rioton; Julien, Andre Maréchal; Mother, Deschamps-Jehin; Father, Lucien Fugere. AMERICAN PREMIERE: Manhattan Opera House, New York City, January 3, 1908. *Cast:* Louise, Mary Garden; Julien, Charles Dalmorès; Mother, Bressler-Gianoli; Father, Charles Gilibert. METROPOLITAN OPERA HOUSE PREMIERE by the Philadelphia-Chicago Opera Company, January 31, 1911. *Cast:* Louise, Mary Garden; Julien, Charles Dalmoras; Mother, Bressler-Gianoli; Father, Hector Dufranne. METROPOLITAN OPERA COMPANY PREMIERE, January 15, 1921. *Cast:* Louise, Geraldine Farrar; Julien, Orville Harrold; Mother, Louise Berat; Father, Clarence Whitehill.

Louise is virtually held prisoner at home

Mary Garden who created the title role in America

Grace Moore sang her first Louise January 28, 1939

Orville Harrold as Julien with Geraldine Farrar as Louise

Hector Dufranne as the Father

Rene Maison as Julien

Vanni-Marcoux as the Father

Mary Gar

Georges Baklanoff as the Father

Ezio Pinza as the Father

Charles Gilibert who sang the role of the Father at the American premiere

Lucia di Lammermoor

BY GAETANO DONIZETTI
Libretto by Salvatore Cammarano

Scotland, 1700. Lord Henry Ashton desires his sister Lucia to marry Lord Arthur Bucklaw, hoping by this wealthy marriage to avoid financial ruin. The unhappy girl has refused and he learns she is in love with Edgar of Ravenswood, his most hated enemy.

In a park near the castle Lucia learns from Edgar that he must go to France. He begs her to let him ask her brother if they cannot first be married, but Lucia is afraid of her brother's hatred. They part promising to remain true to one another.

In Lucia's apartments wedding preparations are being made. Lord Henry hopes to force his sister to marry Lord Arthur. He shows Lucia a forged letter proving Edgar's infidelity, and tells her that he has been implicated in a plot against the king and only this alliance with Lord Arthur will save him. Lucia consents in order to help her brother.

Just as Lucia signs the marriage contracts Edgar rushes in and demands the ceremony cease. Believing Lucia false when he sees her signature on the wedding contract, he departs angrily cursing her and her family. Lord Henry follows and challenges him to a duel.

The wedding night celebrations are interrupted by the wild appearance of the bride who has gone mad and killed her husband. At the end of her ravings among the guests Lucia falls dead.

In the churchyard Edgar waits for Henry and the duel. On learning that the castle bells toll for the dead Lucia he kills himself in remorse.

Luisa Tetrazzini as Lucia

Lucia's wedding festivities

Adelina Patti
as Lucia

The guests at the wedding of Lucia are interrupted by the arrival
of Edgar. They join in the famous sextette

NOTES: WORLD PREMIERE: Teatro Fondo, Naples, Italy, September 26, 1835. *Cast:* Edgar, Gilbert Deuprz; Sir Henry Ashton, Cosselli; Raymond, Porto; Arthur, Giacchini; Norman, Rossi; Alice, Zappucci; Lucia, Fanny Tacchinardi-Persiani. AMERICAN PREMIERE: Theatre D'Orleans, New Orleans, La., May 28, 1841. *Cast:* Edgar, Adolphe Nourrit; Lucia, Julia Calvé. METROPOLITAN OPERA PREMIERE: October 24, 1883. *Cast:* Edgar, Italo Campanini; Sir Henry Ashton, Giuseppe Kaschmann; Arthur, Vincenzo Fornaris; Raymond, Achille Augier; Norman, Amadeo Grassi; Alice, Imogene Forti; Lucia, Marcella Sembrich (debut).

Lucia startles the wedding guests with her mad scene

Nellie Melba
as Lucia

John McCormack
as Edgar

Italo Campanini, the
first Metropolitan
Edgar, October 24,
1883

Tito Schipa
as Edgar

Orville Harrold
as Edgar

James Melton
as Edgar

Josephine Antoine
sang Lucia for first
time at Met,
February 22, 1945

**Thelma Votipka
as Alice**

**Marcella Sembrich made her Met
debut October 24, 1883,
singing Lucia**

**Ferruccio Tagliavini
as Edgar**

**Enrico Caruso sang his first Edgar
at the Met, January 8, 1904**

**Amelita Galli-Curci
as Lucia**

Toti Dal Monte made her American debut at the Met on Dec. 5, 1924, as Lucia

Florence Macbeth as Lucia

Nino Martini as Edgar

Lily Pons made her Met debut as Lucia January 3, 1931

Dolores Wilson made her debut at Met as Lucia, February 8, 1954

Leonard Warren as Lord Ashton

Luisa Tetrazz[i]

[132]

Madame Butterfly

BY GIACOMO PUCCINI
Libretto by Luigi Illica
and Giuseppe Giacosa

Lt. Pinkerton, a United States Navy officer stationed in Japan, wishes to contract a marriage and is assured by the broker that it is binding only as long as he lives with his Japanese wife, and that afterwards she will be free to marry again in accordance with the custom. But his intended bride, Cio-Cio-San, called Madame Butterfly, falls deeply in love with him and believes the contract is entirely binding. The American Consul sees her attitude and begs Pinkerton not to go through with his plan. Pinkerton scoffs and the marriage is arranged. Butterfly shows her trust by giving up her religion and severing ties with her own people. After the ceremony Butterfly's uncle, a priest, curses her for forsaking her religion and the wedding guests depart in haste. Pinkerton comforts his weeping bride as he takes her into their house.

Three years have passed with Pinkerton gone to America. The pathetic and faithful Butterfly still waits for his return. Angrily she upbraids her servant for lack of faith. The consul appears with a letter in which Pinkerton tells him of his marriage and asks him to break the news to Butterfly, but the unhappy man cannot bring himself to tell the grim news. Proudly Butterfly shows the consul the fair-haired son she has borne Pinkerton. After the saddened consul leaves, cannon announce the arrival in the bay of a United States Navy ship. Butterfly decorates the house and prepares to receive her husband.

At dawn Butterfly still waiting for Pinkerton is persuaded to rest. While she sleeps Pinkerton arrives with his new American wife. Butterfly enters to find Mrs. Pinkerton in her garden. She guesses the truth. The American woman wishes to adopt her son, and Butterfly stoically agrees to the request. When Pinkerton returns an hour later for the child he is horrified to find Butterfly dying. She has committed suicide, preferring to die with honor rather than live without it.

**Geraldine Farrar as Cio-Cio-San
about to kill herself**

**Lt. Pinkerton and Cio-Cio-San prepare
for their wedding festivities**

NOTES: WORLD PREMIERE: La Scala. Milan, Italy, February 17,
1904. *Cast:* Cio-Cio-San, Rosina Storchio; Suzuki, Giuseppina Gia-
conia; B. F. Pinkerton, Giovanni Zenatello; Sharpless, Giuseppe
DeLuca. AMERICAN PREMIERE (in English): Belasco Theatre, Wash-
ington, D. C., October 15, 1906, by the H. W. Savage Opera Com-
pany. *Cast:* Cio-Cio-San, Elza Szamosy; Suzuki, Harriet Behne;
B. F. Pinkerton, Joseph F. Sheehan; Sharpless, Winifred Goff.
METROPOLITAN OPERA PREMIERE (in Italian): February 11, 1907.
Cast: Cio-Cio-San, Geraldine Farrar; Suzuki, Louise Homer; B. F.
Pinkerton, Enrico Caruso; Sharpless, Antonio Scotti.

**Lt. Pinkerton's
American wife comes
for Cio-Cio-San's
child. Louise Homer
as Suzuki,
Geraldine Farrar as
Cio-Cio-San,
Helen Mapleson as
Kate Pinkerton**

**Cio-Cio-San and Suzuki prepare for
Lt. Pinkerton's arrival by strewing the room
with flowers**

Amelita Galli-Curci
as Cio-Cio-San

Elsa Szamosy, first Cio-Cio-San in America at
Columbia Theatre, Washington, D. C.,
Oct. 15, 1906

Lucrezia Bori sang
Butterfly in Boston
but never at the Met

Florence Easton
as Cio-Cio-San

Toti Dal Monte
as Cio-Cio-San

Geraldine Farrar, first to sing Madame
Butterfly at Met, Feb. 11, 1907

Edith Mason as Cio-Cio-San

Marion Telva
as Suzuki

Victoria De Los Angeles
as Cio-Cio-San

Licia Albanese as Cio-Cio-San.
Made her Met debut Feb. 9, 1940

Nino Martini
as Lt. Pinkerton

Elisabeth Rethberg
as Cio-Cio-San

Dorothy Kirsten
as Cio-Cio-San

Thomas Chalmers
as Sharpless

Tamaki Miura, Japanese prima
donna, and a famous Cio-Cio-San

Frederick Jagel
as Lt. Pinkerton

The three ladies sigh over the unconscious Tamino

Two priests lead Tamino and Papageno into the temple crypt

The Magic Flute

BY WOLFGANG AMADEUS MOZART
Libretto by Emmanuel Schikaneder and Johann Georg Metzler

Exhausted and fainting, the ancient Egyptian Prince Tamino is lost in a wood and being pursued by a huge serpent when three attendants of the Queen of the Night appear to slay the serpent. Recovering, Tamino sees his servant Papageno dressed as a bird, which he explains is the way to catch birds. He also claims to have killed the serpent. The attendants of the queen punish him for this lie by padlocking his lips. The queen appears to beg Tamino to free her daughter Pamina who is held by the old Priest of Isis, Sarastro. The queen gives Tamino a magic flute and a set of chimes to help him in distress and the Prince and Papageno set off to free the queen's daughter.

In Sarastro's palace Papageno finds the beautiful Pamina and tells her Tamino is coming to rescue her. After some difficulties the prince meets Sarastro who wishes to test his worthiness by passing through the ordeals of the temple.

In a palm grove the priests discuss the case of the lovers. The first ordeal is to be silent under temptation and Tamino passes the test, even when Pamina tempts him and believes his love for her has grown cold.

Pamina is prevented from taking her life because of the heartlessness of the silent Tamino, and Papageno also

wishes to end his life, but instead plays his magic chimes. Suddenly the beautiful Papagena appears before him.

Before barriers of water and a cavern of fire the prince appears, and Pamino finds he now can speak to her. With the aid of the magic flute both pass through fire and water harmlessly. At the temple Tamino and Pamina and Papageno and Papagena are united by Sarastro and live happily ever after.

Papageno and Papagena united at last in the magic garden

The united lovers are hailed by the multitude at the Temple of the Sun

Emmy Destinn as Pamina, Edward Lankow as Sarastro, Leo Slezak as Tamino

Marcella Sembrich as Queen of Night

NOTES: WORLD PREMIERE: Theater auf der Wieden, Vienna, Austria, September 30, 1791. *Cast:* Queen of Night, Hofer; Pamino, Gottlieb; Papagena, Gorl; Tamino, Schack; Monostatos, Gorl; Sarastro, Schikaneder, Sr.; Papageno, Schikaneder, Jr. AMERICAN PREMIERE (in English): Park Theatre, New York City, April 17, 1833. *Cast:* Queen of Night, Mrs. Henry Wallack; Pamino, Mrs. Austin; Sarastro, Charles E. Horn; Papageno, Mr. Placide; Tamino, Mr. Jones; Monostatos, Mr. Fisher; Papagena, Mrs. Sharpe. METROPOLITAN OPERA PREMIERE (in Italian): March 30, 1900. *Cast:* Queen of Night, Marcella Sembrich; Pamino, Emma Eames; Sarastro, Pol Plancon; Papageno, Giuseppe Campaniri; Monostàtos, Antonio Pini-Corsi; Papagena, Zelia de Laussan; Tamino, Andreas Dippel.

Frieda Hempel as Queen of Night

Leo Slezak
as Tamino

Charles Kullman as Tamino

Alexander Kipnis as Sarastro

John Brownlee as Papageno

Bella Alten as Papagena, Otto Goritz as Papageno

Brian Sullivan
as Tamino

Manon pleads with Des Grieux at St. Sulpice

Count Des Grieux invades the gambling salon to admonish his errant son

In Paris, where Manon enjoys a life of luxury with De Bretigny

Manon

BY JULES MASSENET
Libretto by Henri Meilhac
and Philippe Gille

In 1721 a pretty young girl, Manon, on her way to a convent, has stopped at a tavern in Amiens to spend the night with her cousin. While there she captures the imagination of the old minister of finance who makes plans to abduct her in his carriage. The young Chevalier Des Grieux, about to take holy orders, is also attracted by the vivacious girl and, taking the minister's carriage, they elope to Paris.

In Paris Manon lives with Des Grieux who vainly tries to get his father's consent to a wedding. Manon's cousin appears with a rich nobleman, De Bretigny, who tells her that Des Grieux is to be taken away by his father that evening. Attracted by the nobleman's promises of a rich life Manon decides to desert Des Grieux, leaving him deeply in debt. That night, as she starts guiltily, he answers a knock on the door and is seized and carried away.

On a Paris boulevard De Bretigny appears with Manon who now enjoys every luxury. She overhears Des Grieux's father tell De Bretigny that his son is heartbroken over Manon's infidelity and is about to enter a monastery.

At the Seminary of St. Sulpice Des Grieux's father begs him not to become a monk but to marry instead. After he has gone Des Grieux muses sadly about Manon, who suddenly appears before him, begging his forgiveness. She finally persuades him to return to Paris with her.

To satisfy the insatiable demands of Manon Des Grieux gambles heavily and is winning huge stakes at a gambling house until he is accused of cheating. The police enter and arrest Manon and Des Grieux.

On a road near the port of Le Havre her cousin and Des Grieux wait to rescue Manon who is about to be deported. When she finally appears led by soldiers she seems exhausted and ill, but greets Des Grieux joyfully. Asking forgiveness for her unfaithfulness, she dies in his arms.

NOTES: WORLD PREMIERE: Opera Comique, Paris, France, January 19, 1884. *Cast:* Manon, Marie Heilbronn; Des Grieux, Talazac; Lescaut, Taskin; Count Des Grieux, Cobalet; Bretigny, Collin. AMERICAN PREMIERE: Academy of Music, New York City, December 23, 1885. *Cast:* Manon, Minnie Hauk; Des Grieux, Ferruccio Giannini; Lescaut, Giuseppe del Puente; Count Des Grieux, Cherubini; Bretigny, Foscani. METROPOLITAN OPERA PREMIERE (in French): January 16, 1895. *Cast:* Manon, Sybil Sanderson (debut); Des Grieux, Jean de Reszke; Count Des Grieux, Pol Plancon; Lescaut, Mario Ancona; Bretigny, Victor de Gromzeski.

Minnie Hauk sang Manon at its
American premiere

Lucrezia Bori as Manon with Richard Crooks as
Des Grieux

Sybil Sanderson made her Met debut as Manon, January 16, 1895

Marie Heilbronn who
created the role of Manon

Helen Jepson as Manon

Lina Cavalieri, one-time
Spanish dancer who
became a famous opera
singer, as Manon

Mary Garden
as Manon

Anna Fitziu as Manon

Geraldine Farrar as Ma

Frances Alda
as Manon

Enrico Caruso as Des Grieux

In 1928 George Cehanovsky (right) sang De Bretigny at the Met with Giuseppe De Luca, Beniamino Gigli and Lucrezia Bori

Twenty-five years later George Cehanovsky (right) sang De Bretigny at the Met with Martial Singher, Giuseppe Di Stefano and Licia Albanese

Lucien Muratore as Des Grieux

Carl Jorn as Des Grieux

Richard Crooks at Des Grieux

Tito Schipa as Des Grieux

Manon Lescaut and Chevalier Des Grieux declare their love

Manon mourns her lost love

Manon Lescaut

MUSIC AND LIBRETTO BY GIACOMO PUCCINI

A carriage rolls up to an inn at Amiens. The young girl who steps out immediately attracts the handsome Chevalier Des Grieux, who is one of a number of people celebrating in the courtyard. The young girl is Manon Lescaut, and she promises to meet Des Grieux later. An older man named Geronte has also witnessed the arrival and plots to abduct the beautiful girl in his carriage. Instead Manon and Des Grieux elope together in Geronte's coach. Geronte is consoled by thinking it will be easy to lure a vain woman from the poor student Des Grieux.

Manon lives for a time with Des Grieux but deserts him finally for the richer Geronte. Though her surroundings are elegant she is unhappy and longs for her former lover. Geronte attempts to amuse Manon with singers and a dancing master. When she is finally alone Des Grieux appears to find out if she still loves him. As they declare once more their love Geronte enters and angrily sends for the police. Des Grieux begs Manon to escape with him but in her greed to gather all her jewels precious time is lost and she is captured by the police.

At the harbor of Le Havre Manon is waiting to be deported to America as an undesirable. Des Grieux vainly attempts to save her and is overcome with grief as she is herded on board ship. The captain takes pity on him and allows him to come aboard with Manon. Together they sail for America.

In a lonely plain in Louisiana Manon and Des Grieux wander aimlessly, seeking food and a place to rest.

Alarmed by Manon's weakness Des Grieux hurries off alone to find water. Believing she has been deserted Manon sinks exhausted to the ground. Des Grieux returns to find she is dying. He attempts to make her last pitiful moments more comfortable by holding her in his arms.

NOTES: WORLD PREMIERE: Teatro Regio, Turin, Italy, February 1, 1893. *Cast:* Manon, Cesira Ferrani; Des Grieux, Giuseppe Cremonini; Lescaut, Moro; Geronte, Polonini. AMERICAN PREMIERE: Grand Opera House, Philadelphia, Pa., August 29, 1894. *Cast:* Manon, Selma Kort-Krongold; Des Grieux, A. Montegriffo; Lescaut, Warwick Ganor; Geronte, Lodovico Viviani. METROPOLITAN OPERA PREMIERE: January 18, 1907. *Cast:* Manon, Lina Cavalieri; Des Grieux, Enrico Caruso; Lescaut, Antonio Scotti; Geronte, Archangelo Rossi.

Manon is waiting to be deported to America

Enrico Caruso as Des Grieux

Giuseppe De Luca
as Lescaut

Lucrezia Bori made her Met debut singing the title role, November 11, 1912

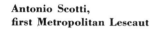

Antonio Scotti,
first Metropolitan Lescaut

Lina Cavalieri,
first Metropolitan Manon Lescaut

Richard Tucker as Des Grieux

Salvatore Baccaloni as Geronte with
Dorothy Kirsten as Manon Lescaut

[151]

Marriage of Figaro

BY WOLFGANG AMADEUS MOZART
Libretto by Lorenzo Da Ponte

Figaro and Susanna, young servants in the house of Count Almaviva and his wife, are discussing their future wedded life together. The old housekeeper Marcellina declares Figaro has promised to marry her and engages a lawyer to press her suit. A page-boy, Cherubino, is in love with the gardener's daughter Barbarina, and seeks Susanna's help in preventing the amorous Count Almaviva from flirting with her. Cherubino hides when the Count enters but is discovered. The Count angrily sends him off to fill a vacancy in his army regiment.

The Countess determines to catch her husband in the act of flirting, and Cherubino is dressed as a girl to deceive him. In the confusion when the Count suddenly demands entrance Cherubino jumps out the window. Figaro attempts to explain to the Count what has happened without incriminating the Countess. Marcellina appears to demand that Figaro keep his promise to marry her. The Count, suspicious of Figaro, postpones his wedding to Susanna for the time being.

By threatening to make Figaro wed the ugly Marcellina, the Count hopes to make Susanna accept his attentions. Susanna pretends to yield and promises to meet him that night in the garden. Marcellina is revealed as Figaro's mother, so the possibility of his marrying her is ended.

Susanna and the Countess disguise themselves as each other, determined to punish the Count and Figaro for their casual ways with women.

In the garden at night Susanna waits for the Count and Figaro watches from a hiding place, hoping to catch her in her supposed infidelity. Cherubino makes love to the Countess thinking she is Barbarina. The Count makes love to his wife, thinking she is Susanna. Figaro makes love to Susanna thinking she is the Countess. In the general confusion of mistaken identities Susanna and the Countess reveal their scheme, the Count admits he has been fooled, and the happy couples return to celebrate the weddings of Susanna and Figaro and Cherubino and Barbarina.

NOTES: WORLD PREMIERE: National Theatre, Vienna, Austria, May 1, 1786. *Cast:* Count, Mandini; Countess, Laschi; Suzanna, Anna Storace; Figaro, Francesco Bennucci; Cherubino, Bussani; Antonio, Francesco Bussani. AMERICAN PREMIERE: Park Theatre, New York City, May 10, 1824. *Cast:* Countess, Miss Johnson; Suzanna, Mrs. Holman; *Figaro,* Pearman; Cherubino, Mrs. Babker; Antonio, Henry Placide. METROPOLITAN OPERA PREMIERE (in Italian): January 31, 1894. *Cast:* Countess, Emma Eames; Cherubino, Sigrid Arnoldson; Susanna, Lillian Nordica; Count Almaviva, Édouard de Reszke; Figaro, Mario Ancona; Bartolo, Antonio Carbone.

Cherubino sings to the Countess, accompanied by Susanna. L-R: Frieda Hempel, Margarete Matzenauer, Geraldine Farrar

**Nadine Conner as Susanna
with Cesare Siepi as Figaro**

**Marcellina, Dr. Bartolo and Don Basilio demand that Figaro
fulfill his obligations**

**Count Almaviva's wife forgives his philanderings
at the happy finale**

**Ezio Pinza as Figaro,
Rise Stevens as Cherubino**

Celebrations for the approaching marriage of Figaro and Susanna

Geraldine Farrar as Cherubino,
Frieda Hempel as the Countess,
Giuseppe De Luca as Figaro

Ezio Pinza
as Figaro

Margarete Matzenauer
as the Countess

Elisabeth Rethberg
as the Countess

Bidu Sayao, Brazilian soprano,
sang her first Susanna at Met
February 20, 1940

Emma Eames as
Countess Almaviva

Jarmila Novotna
as Cherubino

Martial Singher
as Figaro

Salvatore Baccaloni
as Don Bartolo

Margarete Ober,
Giuseppe De Luca,
Enrico Caruso and
Frieda Hempel

Martha

BY FRIEDRICH VON FLOTOW
Libretto by Friedrich Wilhelm Riese

England, during the Reign of Queen Anne. Bored by
court life, Lady Harriet and her companion Nancy decide
to go to a fair at Richmond disguised as servants out for
hire.

Two young farmers, Plunkett and Lionel, have come to
the fair to engage servants. Lionel knows nothing of his
parentage but wears a ring given him by his father with
instructions to present it to the Queen if he is ever in
trouble. The Sheriff announces that any contract for a
servant shall be binding for a year if money is advanced.
When Lady Harriet and Nancy appear disguised as
Martha and Julia they are hired by Lionel and Plunkett
and led away despite their protestations.

The farmers are nonplussed to find they have hired two
such unwilling and ignorant servants, but are so fascinated by their beauty and personality they fall in love. At
night after the men have retired the ladies escape.

The disconsolate Lionel and Plunkett are drinking at an
inn when they are astonished to see Harriet and Nancy
enter with the party of the Queen. When they declare their
love once more the ladies pretend they have never seen
the farmers before and on Harriet's complaint Lionel is
arrested.

When Lionel's ring is presented to the Queen he is revealed as the rightful Earl of Derby, but this change in

his fortunes means nothing to him. He is mentally un-
balanced through grief and love for Lady Harriet. When
Harriet who now returns his love visits him he does not
recognize her.

Nancy and Plunkett and Harriet stage a reproduction of
the Richmond Fair where they all first met. Lionel is
brought forward and seeing them all again is restored to
reason. All ends happily for the two couples.

NOTES: WORLD PREMIERE: Court Theatre, Vienna, Austria, Novem-
ber 25, 1847. *Cast:* Lionel, Joseph Erl; Plunkett, Carl Formes;
Lady Harriet, Anna Zerr; Nancy, Therese Schwartz. AMERICAN
PREMIERE: Niblo's Gardens, New York City, November 1, 1852. *Cast:*
Lionel, Guidi; Harriet, Anna Bishop; Plunkett, Leach; Nancy,
Rosa Jacques. METROPOLITAN OPERA PREMIERE: March 14, 1884.
Cast: Harriet, Marcella Sembrich; Nancy, Zelia Trebelli; Lionel,
Roberto Stagno; Plunkett, Franco Novara.

**Louise Homer
as Nancy**

Giuseppe De Luca
as Plunkett

Kathleen Howard
as Nancy

Frances Alda
as Harriet

Frieda Hempel
as Harriet

Frieda Hempel as Harriet with Margarete Ober
as Nancy

[157]

The Masked Ball

BY GIUSEPPE VERDI
Libretto by Antonio Somma

In Boston near the end of the seventeenth century the Governor is preparing to give a masked ball. His secretary Renato warns him of a conspiracy against his life and the Governor goes in disguise to consult the witch Ulrica about his fate.

Hoping to be able to carry out their plan the conspirators follow him to the witch's hut where Renato's wife Amelia appears to confess to Ulrica her love for the Governor and beg for a magic herb drink to make her forget him. When she has gone Ulrica tells the Governor's fortune. He will be killed by the man who first shakes his hand. Laughing, the Governor holds out his hand to the conspirators who shrink back in fear. Renato enters and grasps his master's hand and the Governor boasts to Ulrica that his secretary is his most trusted friend.

Amelia seeks the magic herb in a lonely spot near Boston. The Governor appears out of the dark, and confessing her love for him she begs him to leave. When her husband Renato enters she quickly veils herself. He warns the Governor the conspirators are approaching to kill him and while he flees Renato escorts his veiled wife back to the city. When her veil is unluckily torn away Renato angrily denounces his wife for infidelity with the Governor. Bitter at his master's supposed affair with his wife the secretary determines to join the conspiracy against the Governor's life.

Renato and the conspirators draw lots to determine who will kill the Governor and Renato is selected. A page comes with invitations to the masked ball.

Though warned by Amelia of his danger the Governor decides to attend the ball in costume and face his enemies. Renato learns from the page how the Governor will be dressed, and in the midst of the festivities stabs him. Before he dies the Governor tells his remorseful servant that Amelia has been guiltless.

Amelia visits Ulrica's den

NOTES: WORLD PREMIERE: Apollo Theatre, Rome, Italy, February 17, 1859. *Cast:* Amelia, Julienne Dejean; Ulrica, Sbriscia; Oscar, Scotti; Richard, Froschini; Renato, Giraldoni;· Samuel, Bassi. AMERICAN PREMIERE: Academy of Music, New York City, February 11, 1861. *Cast:* Amelia, Pauline Colson; Ulrica, Adelaide Phillips; Oscar, Isabella Hinckley; Richard, Pasquale Brignoli; Samuel, Colette. METROPOLITAN OPERA PREMIERE (in German): December 11, 1889. *Cast:* Richard, Julius Perotti; Renato, Theodore Reichmann; Amelia, Lilli Lehmann; Ulrica, Emmy Sonntag-Uhl; Oscar, Betty Frank; Samuel, Josef Arden. Revived in Italian February 23, 1903. *Cast:* Amelia, Johanna Gadski; Ulrica, Louise Homer, Oscar, Fritzi Scheff; Richard, Emelio de Marchi; Renato, Giuseppe Campanari; Samuel, Edouard de Reszke.

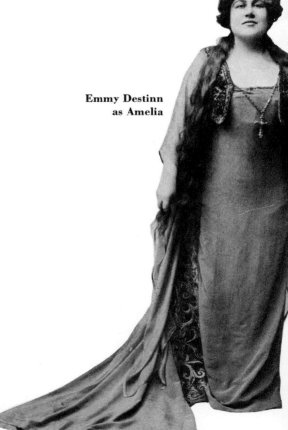

Emmy Destinn as Amelia

Amelia is forced to draw lots

Emma Eames
as Amelia

Pasquale Amato
as Renato

Margaret Harshaw
as Ulrica

Richard Bonelli
as Renato

Renato denounces his wife

Death of the Governor at the Masked Ball

Fritzi Scheff as Oscar,
the page

Mefistofele

MUSIC AND LIBRETTO BY ARRIGO BOÏTO

The Devil Mefistofele pauses en route to Earth, where he hopes to tempt the philosopher Faust, and addresses a few mocking words to the Omnipotent.

In a public square in Frankfurt students are happily celebrating a holiday. Faust, an aged man of great wisdom, notices a strange friar watching him. The sinister appearance of the friar convinces Faust that he is the Devil in disguise.

Back in his study Faust is startled by the sudden appearance of the friar, who drops his cloak and stands revealed as Mefistofele. In return for his lost youth and one hour of happiness Faust agrees to relinquish his soul.

Marguerite and Faust walk alone in her garden while Mefistofele gives her mother a drug to make her sleep. After a passionate love scene, Mefistofele carries Faust to the edge of hell. There the philosopher glimpses the horrors of damnation and is appalled to see a vision of Marguerite chained to the molten rocks.

Marguerite has killed the child she conceived in sin and lies in prison awaiting execution for her crime. Faust enters to rescue her, but the demented girl does not recognize him. When Mefistofele appears Marguerite collapses in terror. Soon she is dead in Faust's arms. The sound of angels is heard announcing her victory over hell.

In Greece Mefistofele tempts Faust with the beautiful Helen of Troy. They embrace ardently while the Devil hurries off once more to Hell.

Once more an old man, Faust reads the Bible in his study. Regretfully he surveys his wasted life and prays to be forgiven for his sins. Mefistofele comes again to tempt him, still hoping to gain his soul, but praying for strength the old man dies. The defeated Devil sinks to Hell while angels bear Faust to Heaven. He, too, has been triumphant in death.

NOTES: WORLD PREMIERE: La Scala, Milan, Italy, March 5, 1868. AMERICAN PREMIERE: Academy of Music, November 24, 1880. *Cast:* Faust, Italo Campanini; Mefistofele, Franco Novara; Martha, Annie Louise Cary; Marguerite and Helen of Troy, Alwina Valleria. METROPOLITAN OPERA PREMIERE: December 5, 1883. *Cast:* Faust, Italo Campinini; Mefistofele, Giuseppe Mirabella; Martha and Pantalis, Zelia Trebelli; Marguerite and Helen of Troy, Christine Nilsson.

Lina Cavalieri
as Helen of Troy

José Mardones
as Mefistofele

Riccardo Martin with Geraldine Farrar

Frances Alda
as Marguerite

Feodor Chaliapin
as Mefistofele

Adamo Didur
as Mefistofele

Walther prepares to audition for the stern Mastersingers

The two couples join Hans Sachs in the famous Quintet

Die Meistersinger

MUSIC AND LIBRETTO BY RICHARD WAGNER

In the German town of Nuremberg in the sixteenth century the knight Walther has fallen in love with Eva, daughter of Pogner. But her father, one of a guild of mastersingers, has promised her hand in marriage to the winner of a song contest. The leading contender for this honor is the presumptuous town clerk Beckmesser. When Walther decides to enter the contest and has a preliminary trial before the assembled mastersingers Beckmesser acts as his 'marker' and gives him so many bad marks that his chances of winning Eva seem very slim and the mastersingers reject him.

On a beautiful summer evening the poet and philosopher Hans Sachs, sitting before his cobbler shop musing on the beauty of the rejected Walther's song, is told by his neighbor Eva that she intends to elope with the knight no matter who wins the contest. The lovers are about to go off together when Beckmesser arrives to serenade Eva beneath her window. Hans Sachs punctuates the mistakes in Beckmesser's serenade by pounding on a shoe with his hammer. The noise wakens the neighborhood and the street becomes a riot of people. Sachs takes Walther into his home as Eva slips into her own. When the town night-watchman approaches on his rounds the town is peaceful again.

Before the contest Walther shows Hans Sachs the poem he will sing at the contest. After they have left the room together Beckmesser enters and seeing Walther's verses thinks they have been written by the poet Sachs. He slips them into his pocket with the intention of using them himself at the song contest.

In a nearby field the townspeople gather for the song contest. In a great parade the various guilds and mastersingers march onto the field. Beckmesser is the first to perform, making such a fiasco of his song that he is laughed away. Walther then sings his prize song, and recognizing his superiority and artistry, the mastersingers admit him to their guild and award him the first place, as well as the hand of Eva.

NOTES: WORLD PREMIERE: Royal Court Theatre, Munich, Germany, June 21, 1868. *Cast:* Hans Sachs, Franz Betz; Pogner, Bousewein; Beckmesser, Hoelzel; Walther, Franz Nachbaur; Eva, Mathilde Mallinger; Magdalene, Liez. AMERICAN PREMIERE: Metropolitan Opera Company, New York City, January 4, 1886. *Cast:* Hans Sachs, Emil Fischer; Pogner, Josef Staudigl; Beckmesser, Otto Kemlitz; Walther, Albert Stritt; Eva, Auguste Seidl-Kraus; Magdalene, Marianne Brandt.

Beckmesser prepares his song for the Mastersingers and townsfolk

Auguste Seidl-Kraus and Emil Fischer who sang Eva
and Hans Sachs at the American premiere, January 4, 1886

Anton Van Rooy as Hans Sachs

Auguste Seidl-Kraus as Eva

Emil Fischer made his last
appearance at the Met
as Hans Sachs
March 15, 1907

Louise Homer as Magdalene

Eleanor Steber as Eva

Johanna Gadski as Eva

Rene Maison
who made his Met debut as Walth
February 3, 1936

Herbert Janssen
as Hans Sachs

Lotte Lehmann
as Eva

Friedrich Schorr
as Hans Sachs

Emmy Destinn as Eva

stin Thorborg as Magdalene

George Meader as David

Hermann Weil and Otto Goritz as
Hans Sachs and Beckmesser

Ernst Van Dyck
as Walther

Charles Kullman
as Walther

Andreas Dippel
as Walther

Mignon

BY CHARLES LOUIS AMBROISE THOMAS
Libretto by Michel Carré and Jules Barbier

As a child, Mignon was taken from her father, an Italian nobleman named Lothario, by a band of gypsies. The tragedy has deranged the old Lothario and he spends his life wandering in search of his daughter as a travelling minstrel. His travels take him into Germany where, having forgotten his real name and home, he seeks refuge at an inn. In the courtyard a group of gypsies try to force Mignon, now grown, to dance for them. When she refuses, Lothario, not knowing who she is, tries to protect her from the anger of the gypsy leader. A young student, Wilhelm Meister, saves them both from harm and buys Mignon's freedom from the gypsy band. Dressing her as a boy to use as his page Wilhelm takes her with him to a nearby castle in company with a troupe of strolling players, one of whom, Philine, is infatuated with him.

Unhappy over his interest in Philine, Mignon tries to emulate the beautiful actress by dressing up in borrowed finery. When Philine laughs at her the humiliated Mignon runs away and attempts to drown herself, but is prevented by the old man Lothario. Wishing to help Mignon revenge herself on Philine, Lothario sets fire to the castle. Realizing Mignon is in danger, Wilhelm rushes to her rescue.

Lothario and Mignon have been brought by Wilhelm to Italy where the girl begins to recover from a dangerous illness. While caring for her Wilhelm comes to the realization that he loves her deeply, but Mignon cannot believe that he has entirely forgotten his brilliant actress Philine. Finding himself in strangely familiar surroundings Lothario's lost memories come crowding back once more. He is Count Lothario, and only the absence of his daughter Sperata mars his happiness. At the mention of the name Mignon recognizes that she is his lost daughter. With father and daughter at last happily reunited, Wilhelm and Mignon become engaged with the old man's blessing.

NOTES: WORLD PREMIERE: Opera Comique, Paris, France, November 17, 1866. *Cast:* Mignon, Celestine Galli-Marie; Philine, Marie Gabel; Wilhelm Meister, Leon Achard; Lothario, Batailli; Frederic, Voisy. AMERICAN PREMIERE (in Italian): Academy of Music, New York City, November 22, 1871. *Cast:* Mignon, Christine Nilsson; Philine, Leon Duval; Wilhelm Meister, Victor Capoul; Lothario, Jamet: Frederic, Ronconi. METROPOLITAN OPERA PREMIERE (in Italian): October 31, 1883. *Cast:* Mignon, Christine Nilsson; Philine, Alwina Valleria; Wilhelm Meister, Victor Capoul; Lothario, Giuseppe del Puente; Frederic, Sofia Scalchi.

Wilhelm saves Mignon and Lothario from the anger of the gypsy leader

Risë Stevens as Mignon, Giuseppe di Stefano as Wilhelm

Patrice Munsel made her Met debut
as Philine January 4, 1946

Clotilde Bressler-Gianoli
as Mignon

Sofia Scalchi,
first
Metropolitan Frederic

Christine Nilsson,
first Met Mignon

Maggie Teyte
as Mignon

[167]

Luisa Tetrazzini
as Philine

Marion Talle
as Philine

Alessio de Paolis as Laerte

Geraldine Farrar
as Mignon

Gladys Swarthout
as Mignon

Richard Crooks
as Wilhelm

Risë Stevens
as Mignon

Lillian Nordica as Philine

Armand Tokatyan
as Wilhelm

Patrice Munsel sings "Je suis Titania, la blonde"

Ezio Pinza as Lothario

[169]

Norma professes her love for the Roman, Pollione

Norma confesses her guilt to the Druids

Norma

BY VINCENZO BELLINI
Libretto by Felice Romani

In a sacred grove the Druids wait for their High Priestess Norma to declare war against an invading army of Romans. But unknown to the Druids Norma has broken her sacred vows and secretly married the Roman Proconsul Pollione, to whom she has borne two children. Rebuking the Druids for the martial attitude she sings a hymn to peace.

The Roman Pollione has tired of Norma and loves the priestess Adalgisa, whom he secretly urges to leave with him and come to Rome. At first she promises to go with him, but filled with remorse, later confesses to Norma that she has loved a Roman and begs to be forgiven. The sympathetic Norma offers to help her escape until she learns Adalgisa's lover is Pollione. With passionate hatred she cries for vengeance.

Norma determines to kill Pollione's two sleeping children, but coming on them as they sleep she is unable to carry out her intention. Instead she prepares to give up both Pollione and her children to Adalgisa and herself seek death on the funeral pyre. Moved by this expression of sacrifice Adalgisa vainly attempts to beg Pollione to return to his first love.

In the sacred temple Pollione tries to force Adalgisa to return with him to Rome, but Norma interrupts them. The enraged priestess summons her people and urges them to war against the Romans. When Pollione is discovered in the ranks of the soldiers he is brought forth as a spy and Norma prepares to give judgment. But she is unable to bring herself to plunge a dagger into the man she loves. She will allow him instead to return unharmed to Rome if he will give up Adalgisa. Pollione refuses, and Norma at last confesses her own guilt to the flabbergasted Druids and claims atonement in death on the funeral pyre. Deeply moved by this expression of devotion Pollione begs to be allowed to die with Norma. Together the two reunited lovers ascend the funeral pyre.

NOTES: WORLD PREMIERE: La Scala, Milan, Italy, December 26, 1831. *Cast:* Norma, Giuditta Pasta; Adalgisa, Giulia Grisi; Pollione, Donzelli. AMERICAN PREMIERE (in English): Chestnut Theatre, Philadelphia, Pa., January 11, 1841. *Cast:* Norma, Mary Ann Wood; Pollione, Joseph Wood; Oroveso, William Francis Brough; Adalgisa, Charlotte Wilson Bailey. METROPOLITAN OPERA PREMIERE (in German): February 27, 1890. *Cast:* Norma, Lilli Lehmann; Pollione, Paul Kalisch; Adalgisa, Betty Frank; Oroveso, Emil Fischer; Flavio, Albert Mittelhause; Clotilde, Louise Meisslinger.

Zinka Milanov as Norma

Rosa Ponselle in óne of her most famous roles

Rosa Raisa as Norma

Stella Roman. as Norma

Louise Homer as Orpheus

Orfeo ed Euridice

BY CHRISTOPH WILLIBALD VON GLUCK

Libretto by Ranieri Calzabigi

At her tomb Orpheus laments over the death of his bride, the beautiful Eurydice. Deeply touched by his grief, Amor the God of Love proposes to allow Orpheus to descend into the underworld to seek Eurydice. There is one condition, however, if Orpheus is to have his wife back again in the realm of the living. If Pluto, God of the Underworld, is moved by his plea and allows Eurydice to go back with her husband, Orpheus must never look at Eurydice's face until after they have recrossed the river Styx. If he should turn back to look upon her she must return at once to the dead. Imploring the aid of the Gods Orpheus sets out after his wife.

At the entrance to the Underworld the furies attempt to frighten Orpheus, but soon become moved by the beauty of his song and the pity of his grief. He continues down into the terrible realm.

In the Elysian fields where the good spirits seek rest and contentment Orpheus finds his bride surrounded by happy shades. Taking Eurydice by the hand, but careful not to look upon her face, he gently leads her from the valley.

As they approach nearer and nearer to the upper world Eurydice's wonder and unhappiness increase. She believes Orpheus no longer loves her, as he never once looks upon her face. Hurrying on ahead Orpheus begs her to follow, but Eurydice unhappily declares that she would prefer to remain among the dead than live without the love of her husband. She cries out in such sorrow that, in a moment of forgetfulness, Orpheus looks back upon her. Immediately she falls lifeless. Happily, the God Amor hears Orpheus' heartrending song of pathos and is so deeply moved that he permits the two lovers to return together to the world above.

The Temple of Love

NOTES: WORLD PREMIERE: Hofburgtheater, Vienna, Austria, October 5, 1762. AMERICAN PREMIERE (in English): Winter Garden, May 25, 1863. *Cast:* Orpheus, Felicita Vestvali; Eurydice, Johanna Rotter; Amor, Mina Geory. METROPOLITAN OPERA PREMIERE (in Italian): December 30, 1891. *Cast:* Ornheus, Giulia Ravogli; Euridyce, Sophia Ravogli; Amor, Mathilde Bauermeister.

Eugenia Mantelli as Orpheus

Orpheus (Kerstin Thorborg), Eurydice (Irene Jessner) and Amore (Marisa Morel)

Orpheus and Eurydice are reunited

Otello

BY GIUSEPPE VERDI
Libretto by Arrigo Boïto

Returning to his palace in Cyprus after wars with the Turks the victorious commander Otello is welcomed by the rejoicing populace. Iago, one of his officers, hates Otello for promoting another officer, Cassio. Hoping to discredit Cassio, Iago and his confidant Rodrigo scheme to get Cassio drunk. During a brawl which follows, the intoxicated Cassio wounds Montano, Otello's predecessor as Governor of Cyprus. The noise brings Otello who angrily deprives Cassio of his command.

The crafty Iago suggests to Cassio that he ask Otello's wife Desdemona to beg him to restore Cassio to rank. In the meantime Iago begins to insinuate to Otello that his wife is unfaithful to him with Cassio. He says Cassio has in his possession a handkerchief which had been a gift of Otello to his wife. The enraged Moor is consumed with jealousy.

When Desdemona pleads for Cassio, Otello's doubts increase. He overhears Cassio and Iago conversing about Cassio's sweetheart in such a way that Otello believes they are speaking of Desdemona. When the handkerchief is produced, apparently from Cassio's room, Otello is convinced of his wife's infidelity. Insanely jealous, he determines to kill her, allowing Iago to take care of Cassio.

The Venetian Ambassador arrives with news that Otello has been promoted to another command, and that Cassio is to be Governor of Cyprus. In front of the assembled throng Otello denounces his wife. She is dumbfounded by his behavior.

The heartsick Desdemona prepares to retire, though she is too apprehensive at first to fall asleep. Gently Otello steals into her chamber and wakens her with a kiss. He confronts her with the story and though she vainly protests her innocence, at last strangles her to death. Her screams arouse the palace and the treachery of Iago is soon exposed. The broken-hearted and remorseful Otello realizes the complete innocence of his wife, and in anguish draws a dagger and stabs himself to death.

NOTES: WORLD PREMIERE: La Scala, Milan, Italy, February 5, 1887. *Cast:* Otello, Francesco Tamagno; Iago, Victor Maurel; Cassio, Giovanni Paroli; Desdemona, Romilda Pantaleoni; Emilia, Ginevra Petrovich. AMERICAN PREMIERE: Academy of Music, New York City, April 16, 1888. *Cast:* Otello, Francesco Marconi; Iago, Antonio Galassi; Cassio, di Comis; Desdemona, Eva Tetrazzini; Emilia, Sofia Scalchi. METROPOLITAN OPERA PREMIERE: January 11, 1892. *Cast:* Otello, Jean de Reszke; Iago, Eduardo Camera; Cassio, Victor Capoul; Desdemona, Emma Albani; Emilia, Sofia Scalchi.

Frances Alda as Desdemona with Leo Slezak as Otello

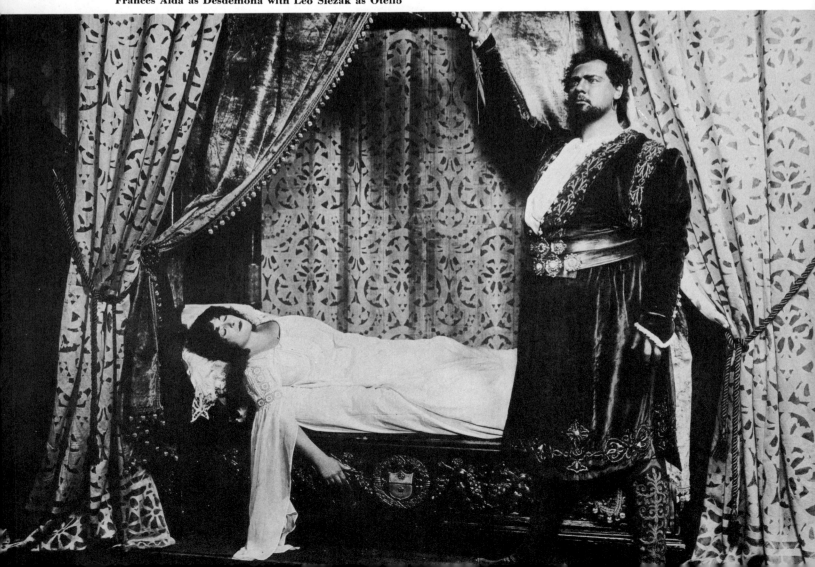

Iago plants suspicion in Otello's mind

Desdemona is murdered by Otello

Giovanni Zenatello as Otello

Lawrence Tibbett as Iago, Giovanni Martinelli as Otello

Emma Albani as Desdemona

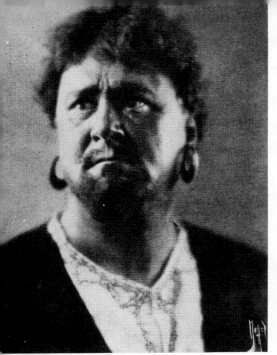

Charles Marshall

Ramon Vinay

FAMOUS OTELLOS

Nicola Zerola

Francesco Tan

Giovanni Martinelli

Leo Slezak made his Met debut in the role
November 17, 1909

[176]

Marie Rappold as Desdemona

Eleanor Steber as Desdemona

Frances Alda as Desdemona

Lawrence Tibbett
as Iago

Victor Maurel created Iago
at the world premiere and first sang
it at the Met December 3, 1894

Emma Calvé as Desdemona

Joseph Schwartz
as Iago

Emma Eames as Desdemona

Antonio Scotti, Florence Wickham, Frances Alda and Leo Slezak

The strolling players begin their Harlequinade

The townsfolk are enthralled

I Pagliacci

MUSIC AND LIBRETTO BY RUGGIERO LEONCAVALLO

A group of strolling players come into a small Italian village. Their leader Canio invites the villagers to attend their performance that evening. Some of the performers go off to a tavern leaving Canio's wife Nedda alone. One of the actors, a deformed hunchback named Tonio, declares his love for Nedda. Though she laughs at him, he continues to annoy her. Angrily she strikes him with a whip. He swears vengeance, and soon spies on Nedda and Silvio, a young peasant, when they make love secretly. Silvio wants Nedda to run away with him that night. Tonio, hearing this information, rushes off to tell Canio. When Canio returns and overhears Nedda and Silvio he is maddened by jealousy. Though Silvio escapes unseen, Canio demands to know the name of his wife's lover. She refuses to tell, and the clown is heartbroken and bitter over his wife's infidelity.

In the evening a crowd of villagers wait for the play to begin. While Nedda collects money from the audience she manages to caution Silvio against Canio's jealousy. The play begins. Nedda, as Columbine, awaits her lover, Harlequin, while her husband, played by Canio, is away. Instead of Harlequin, Tonio, as the dupe Taddeo, enters and attempts to make love in his grotesque way. Hearing her lover at the window Columbine rushes the dull Taddeo out of the room. Harlequin and Columbine are dining together when Taddeo hurries back in with news that Columbine's husband is coming. The lover escapes, and the angry husband demands to know who he is. The audience begins to be aware the intense scene is not all acting. Deadly serious, Canio seizes a knife from the table and stabs Nedda. As she falls she cries out for help to Silvio, in the audience. As the discovered lover rushes to her aid he is stabbed in turn by the maddened clown. Stupefied, Canio addresses the horror-stricken crowd. "The comedy is ended."

Antonio Scotti as Tonio

NOTES: WORLD PREMIERE: Teatro dal Verma, Milan, Italy, May 21, 1892. *Cast:* Canio, Giraud; Tonio, Victor Maurel; Nedda, Adelina Stehle; Silvio, Mario Ancona; Beppe, F. Daddi. AMERICAN PREMIERE: Grand Opera House, New York City, June 15, 1893. *Cast:* Canio, Montigriffo; Tonio, Giuseppe Campanari; Nedda, Selma Kort-Krongold; Silvio, Perry Averill; Beppe, di Pasquali. METROPOLITAN OPERA PREMIERE: December 11, 1893. *Cast:* Canio, Fernando de Lucia; Tonio, Mario Ancona; Nedda, Nellie Melba; Silvio, Edmondo Gromzeski; Beppe, Pedro Guetary.

**Amadeo Bassi
as Canio**

**Geraldine Farrar
as Nedda**

Enrico Caruso as Canio, one of his most popular roles

Canio (Giovanni Martinelli) hails his audience

Alma Gluck as Nedda

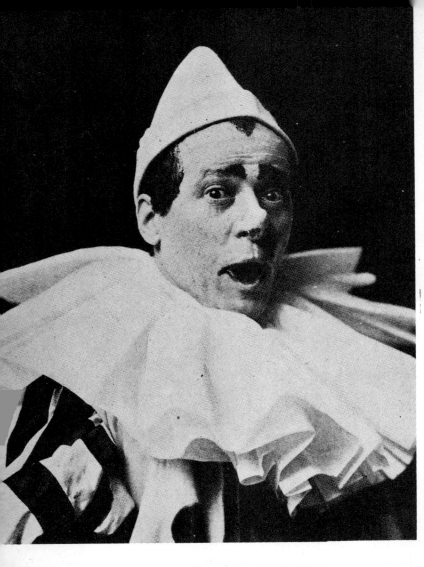

Giuseppe Campanari,
first to sing Tonio
in America

Giovanni Martinelli
wearing Pagliacci
costume Caruso
presented him

Edward Johnson
as Canio

Gino Penno
as Canio

Lucien Muratore
as Canio

Fritzi Scheff as Nedda.
Paderewski called her
"the little devil of
grand opera."

[182]

Paul Althouse
as Canio

Albert Alvarez
as Canio

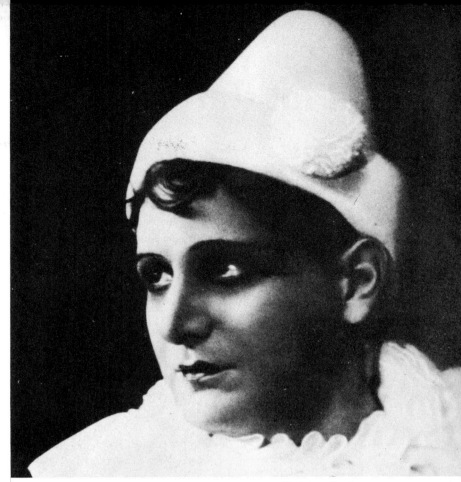

Giacomo Lauri-Volpi as Canio

Claudia Muzio
as Nedda

John Charles Thomas
as Tonio

Florence Easton
as Nedda

Lauritz Melchior
as Canio

Parsifal

MUSIC AND LIBRETTO BY RICHARD WAGNER

The cup which caught the blood of Christ on the cross and the spear which pierced his side were found by Titurel and are guarded by him and the Knights of the Holy Grail at their temple at Montsalvat in the mountains of Spain. The old Titurel appointed his son Amfortas as Keeper of the Grail. The magician Klingsor, angry for not being made a knight with the others, has built an enchanted castle and garden nearby, aided by Kundry, the woman who laughed at Christ on the cross. Enchanting and tempting Amfortas in the magic garden Kundry caused him to be wounded by the sacred spear. He cannot die nor can he be cured until the wound is touched by the sacred spear in the hands of a guileless fool. Near the castle of the knights, Kundry sinks exhausted and penitent. Though she hopes to be able to cure Amfortas he does not hope to be healed until the coming of the guileless one. At this moment the young hunter Parsifal appears. He is invited to go into the Temple of the Holy Grail.

In the temple Amfortas is brought in on a litter for the feast of Communion, and the Holy Grail is unveiled. Parsifal watches the ceremony mutely.

Knowing his power is threatened by Parsifal's innocence, Klingsor wakens Kundry from her sleep and orders her to tempt Parsifal into the magic gardens. Parsifal enters the garden but resists temptation and denounces Kundry. Klingsor appears and hurls his magic spear at Parsifal, but it hangs miraculously in mid-air and is seized by Parsifal. Immediately the garden and castle and Klingsor disappear, and Kundry falls fainting to the ground.

Many years later Parsifal returns from wide travels to Montsalvat, still carrying the sacred spear. The degraded and repentant Kundry washes his feet and dries them with her hair. Bells call the knights to Good Friday prayers. In the temple the Holy Grail is once more revealed, after the suffering Amfortas is carried in on his litter. Parsifal enters to touch Amfortas' wound with the sacred spear, and he is miraculously healed. Kundry dies forgiven, and Parsifal is hailed as the new keeper of the Holy Grail.

Parsifal meets Gurnemanz in the forest

The Holy Grail is brought before Amfortas as Parsifal watches mutely

The flower maidens try to tempt Parsifal

NOTES: WORLD PREMIERE: Bayreuth, Germany, July 28, 1882. *Cast:* Parsifal, Hermann Winkelmann; Amfortas, Theodor Reichmann; Titurel, August Kindermann; Klingsor, Carl Hill; Gurnemanz, Emil Scaria; Kundry, Amalia Materna. AMERICAN PREMIERE: Metropolitan Opera House, New York City, December 24, 1903. *Cast:* Kundry, Milka Ternina; Parsifal, Alois Burgstaller; Amfortas, Anton Van Rooy; Gurnemanz, Robert Blass; Klingsor, Otto Goritz; Titurel, Marcel Journet.

After years of wandering, the knight Parsifal returns still carrying the sacred spear

The death of Kundry

Orville Harrold with Margarete Matzenauer

Amalia Materna who created the role of Kundry

Anton Van Rooy sang Amfortas at the American premiere

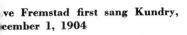

...ve Fremstad first sang Kundry, ...cember 1, 1904

Emil Scaria, the first Gurnemanz

Milka Ternina, first to sing Kundry in America

Alois Burgstaller sang Parsifal at the American premiere

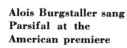

[187]

Lillian Nordica as Kundry

Ernst Van Dyck as Parsifal

Louise Homer as Kundry

Martial Singher as Amfortas

Sigurd Bjorling as Amfortas

Alexander Kipnis made his Met debut as Gurnemanz, January 5, 1940

Lauritz Melchior as Parsifal

Margarete Matzenauer
as Kundry

Clarence Whitehill
as Amfortas

Andreas Dippel as Parsifal

Pelleas
et Melisande

BY CLAUDE ACHILLE DEBUSSY
Libretto by Maurice Maeterlinck

In ancient times Melisande is combing her long golden hair by a fountain in a deep forest. Golaud, a mighty hunter, comes upon her and is fascinated by her strange beauty and decides to marry her and take her home with him.

In the gloomy castle of old King Arkel, Golaud's mother learns that he has married a strange and beautiful woman and will soon return with her to his home. His young brother Pelleas places a light in the castle window to welcome the couple. In the gardens Melisande is depressed by the gloominess of the castle. Her unhappiness increases when she learns that the passionate and handsome Pelleas is leaving on the morrow.

Beside a pool Pelleas and Melisande meet. They are in love, and in her playfulness she drops her wedding ring into a deep pool where it cannot be recovered. Golaud is mysteriously thrown from his horse and wounded at the exact moment Melisande lost her ring. She nurses him back to health.

Surprising Pelleas and Melisande together, Golaud upbraids them for acting like children. Pelleas is warned by his brother to be less attentive to Melisande, who is about to give birth to a child.

Pelleas and Melisande sadly agree to part, but when Golaud comes unexpectedly upon them he mistreats Melisande. The aged King Arkel does not believe that the strange girl has long to live. He believes in her innocence and will not let Golaud handle her roughly. Alone, Melisande admits to Pelleas that she loves him. As they embrace Golaud is watching. He rushes in and slays Pelleas with his sword.

Melisande has given birth to a little girl, but her own life is in grave danger. The others gather about the bedside realizing she is dying. Melisande forgives the remorseful Golaud. After she has gone, the old King Arkel takes Melisande's child in his arms. A life is ended, another life begins.

NOTES: WORLD PREMIERE: Opera Comique, Paris, France, April 30, 1902. AMERICAN PREMIERE: Manhattan Opera House, February 19, 1908. *Cast:* Arkel, M. Arimondi; Pelleas, Jean Perier; Golaud, Hector Dufranne; Melisande, Mary Garden; Genevieve, Gerville-Reache. METROPOLITAN OPERA PREMIERE: March 21, 1925. *Cast:* Melisande, Lucrezia Bori; Genevieve, Kathleen Howard; Pelleas, Edward Johnson; Golaud, Clarence Whitehill; Arkel, Leon Rothier.

Edward Johnson, first to sing Pelleas at the Met

**Theodor Uppman
as Pelleas**

**Pelleas declares his love for
Melisande**

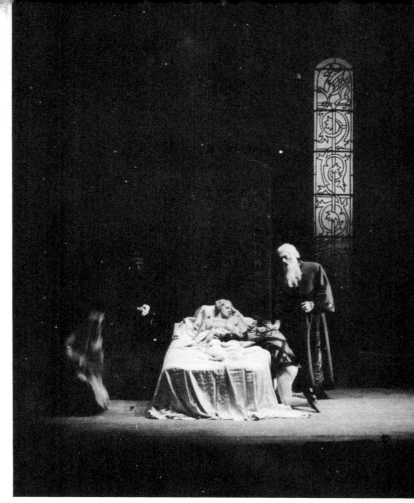

Melisande's death

**Lucrezia Bori, the Met's first
Melisande**

The lovers at the tower

**Charles Dalmores
as Pelleas**

**Emma Trentini
as Little Yniold**

**Mary Garden who created the
role in Paris, April 30, 1902**

Jeanne Gerville-Reache,
first American Genevieve

Hector Dufranne,
first American Golaud

Maggie Teyte as
Melisande, one of her
famous roles

Margaret Harshaw
as Genevieve

Martial Singher
as Pelleas

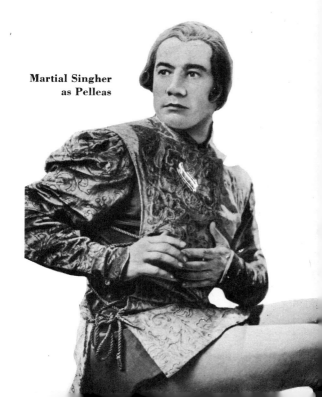

Peter Ibbetson

BY DEEMS TAYLOR
Libretto by Constance Collier and Deems Taylor

Into the festivities at Mrs. Deane's country ball comes the egotistical Colonel Ibbetson to read a poem he offers as his own. Peter Ibbetson reveals the fraud, for the poem is in reality not original. Colonel Ibbetson quarrels with Peter, whom he claims as a natural son. After the Colonel has left, Peter speaks of his childhood, of the pleasant days spent in the garden at Passy with his parents and the beloved Mimsey, a companion of his youth. Where are they all now, he wonders, and in a dream he sees the garden again, and the familiar faces. The Duchess of Towers enters and seems to recognize Peter as her own playmate of long ago. Peter is mesmerized by her likeness to the long-lost Mimsey, but is too shy to speak.

Revisiting childhood haunts in Paris, Peter is disappointed to find the precious landmarks gone. As he rests on a couch at an inn he sees the Duchess of Towers drive by in the street. In a dream he is reunited again with the beloved Mimsey, but the dream is shattered by the vision of Colonel Ibbetson, attacking his mother. Peter wakes to find the Duchess of Towers in the room. They reveal their identities, and Peter embraces his Mimsey once again. But soon the Duchess must go, never to see Peter again.

Colonel Ibbetson and Peter quarrel over the Colonel's claim that Peter is his natural son. In anger Peter strikes the elderly man with a cane and kills him. In jail and under sentence of death Peter refuses to offer any explanation of why he attacked the Colonel, though a confession might soften his punishment. The death sentence is not carried out, but Peter must remain a prisoner for life. In anguish, he dreams again of Mimsey and the scenes of his childhood.

Forty years later, Peter lies ill and dying, having heard that the Duchess is dead. Once more he dreams of his childhood, and as he dies, he is reunited forever with his beloved Mimsey, the Duchess of Towers.

NOTES: WORLD PREMIERE: Metropolitan Opera House, New York, N. Y., February 7, 1931. *Cast:* Peter Ibbetson, Edward Johnson; Colonel Ibbetson, Lawrence Tibbet; Mary, Lucrezia Bori; Mrs. Deane, Marion Telva.

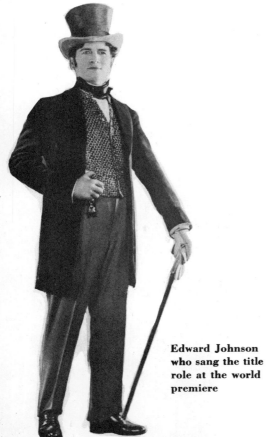

Lucrezia Bori who created the role of the Duchess of Towers in the opera

Edward Johnson who sang the title role at the world premiere

Mrs. Deane's country ball

Le Prophète

BY GIACOMO MEYERBEER
Libretto by Eugène Scribe

Holland, 1536. Bertha wishes to marry John of Leyden and goes with his mother Fides to obtain the consent of Count Oberthal, to whom she is a vassel. Bertha and Fides make their plea, but the count is so struck with Bertha's beauty that he claims her for himself, and the two women are held prisoner.

At an inn a group of Anabaptists preparing a revolt are struck with John's resemblance to David. They beseech him to become their prophet. Bertha, having escaped, rushes in begging to be saved, and is hidden just as the count enters seeking her. He threatens to kill Fides unless Bertha is produced immediately. Torn between love for sweetheart and mother, John finally gives Bertha to the tyrant. Hesitating no longer, he agrees to join the Anabaptists as their prophet, and leaves a bloody garment for his mother so that she will think he has been killed.

In the Anabaptist camp John learns from Count Oberthal, who has been taken prisoner, that Bertha still lives and is held in the city of Munster. He prepares to attack the city at once.

In the Munster public square John governs the city as a prophet, feared and hated by the people. His mother Fides begs in the streets, and is met there by Bertha. Learning from Fides of her son's supposed death at the hands of the Anabaptists, Bertha believes the Prophet is guilty of killing her lover. She swears to have revenge.

The Prophet is about to be crowned in the cathedral. As he enters, his mother rushes forward recognizing him. Knowing it would be disastrous to acknowledge her, John denounces her and she is led away to prison.

The Prophet visits his mother in jail, and she scorns him for his many crimes. Just as he repents and begs forgiveness, Bertha enters by a secret passage, intending to kill the Prophet. When she realizes the Prophet is her lover John she is horror-stricken at the thought of his wickedness. Stabbing herself, she dies cursing his name.

In the great hall John learns the Anabaptists intend to betray him. When they are all assembled at a banquet he secretly gives a signal. There is a terrible explosion and fire as John, his mother, and his enemies perish together.

NOTES: WORLD PREMIERE: Paris Opera House, Paris, France, April 16, 1849. AMERICAN PREMIERE: New Orleans, La., April 2, 1850. METROPOLITAN OPERA PREMIERE: March 21, 1884. *Cast:* Bertha, Alwina Valleria; John of Leyden, Roberto Stagno; Zacharias, Giovanni Mirabelle; Jonas, Signor Stagi; Fides, Sofia Scalchi (debut).

Enrico Caruso as John of Leyden

Enrico Caruso as John with Margarete Matzenauer as Fides

Erda, the earth-goddess, rises out of the ground and prophesies doom

Das Rheingold

MUSIC AND LIBRETTO BY RICHARD WAGNER

At the bottom of the Rhine three maidens guard the Rheingold. They fascinate Alberich, one of a race of dwarfs called Nibelungs. Foolishly the maidens reveal their secret to Alberich. Whoever fashions a magic ring from the Rheingold can rule the world. Only one power will be denied him, the power of love. Snatching the Rheingold from them, Alberich leaves the maidens to mourn their loss.

The giants have built a magnificent castle called Valhalla for the gods atop the mountains. Wotan, chief of the gods, is triumphant, but his wife Fricka reminds him of the price he must pay for the work of the giants. He must give them the goddess of youth, Freia. Wotan attempts to get out of his bargain but the giants Fasolt and Fafner insist. With the goddess of youth gone the gods begin to age rapidly. The God Loge suggests a plan to get Freia back. If they can steal the Rheingold from Alberich, they could trade the gold for the goddess of youth.

Alberich has fashioned a magic ring and rules omnipotently. He has made a magic helmet with which he can assume any shape. Wotan and Loge come seeking the Rheingold and the ring. The wily Loge doubts the power of Alberich's helmet, and the dwarf demonstrates by changing into a dragon, then into a toad. Wotan steps on the toad while Loge appropriates the helmet. When Alberich resumes his natural shape he is bound up and carried off by the gods.

At Valhalla the gods demand the ring from Alberich, which at last he is forced to part with. But doing so he curses it and declares that its owner shall have nothing but misfortune. When the giants come demanding the Rheingold the gods willingly part with it. But Wotan is loathe to give up the ring, until the earth mother Erda rises out of the ground to warn Wotan of Alberich's curse. Reluctantly Wotan parts with the ring, and immediately the power of the curse is demonstrated. The giants Fasolt and Fafner quarrel over possession of the ring and Fasolt is slain. As the gods enter Valhalla the Rheinmaidens are heard crying over their loss.

The Giants return
Freia to the Gods

David Bispham
as Alberich

Ernst Van Dyck

Emil Fischer sang Wotan
at the American premiere

Margarete Matzenauer
as Fricka, Hermann
Weil as Wotan

NOTES: WORLD PREMIERE: Royal Court Theatre, Munich, Germany, September 9, 1869. *Cast:* Wotan, August Kindermann; Donner, Heinrich; Froh, Nachbar; Loge, Heinrich Vogl; Alberich, Fischer; Mime, Max Schlosser; Fasolt, Polzer; Fafner, Bausewein; Fricka, Sophie Stehle; Freia, Muller; Erda, Seehofer; Woglinde, Kaufmann; Wellgunde, Thersa Vogl; Flosshilde, Ritter. AMERICAN PREMIERE: Metropolitan Opera Company, New York City, January 4, 1889. *Cast:* Wotan, Emil Fischer; Loge, Max Alvary; Donner, Alois Grienauer; Froh, Albert Mittelhauser; Alberich, Joseph Beck; Mime, Wilhelm Sedlmayer; Fafner, Eugene Weiss; Fasolt, Ludwig Modlinger; Fricka, Fanny Moran-Olden; Freia, Katti Bettaque; Woglinde, Sophie Traubmann; Wellgunde, Felicie Kaschowska; Flosshilde and Erda, Hedwig Reil.

Monterone rebukes the wanton Duke

Rigoletto

BY GIUSEPPE VERDI
Libretto by Francesco Maria Piave

In Mantua in the sixteenth century the profligate young Duke falls in love with every pretty face he sees. The disgruntled nobles plan to have revenge on him and his mocking jester Rigoletto, who is suspected of having a sweetheart. Old Count Monterone, whose daughter has been defiled by the Duke, denounces him and is mocked by Rigoletto. Monterone utters a curse on the deformed jester which makes a deep impression on Rigoletto, as he fears for the safety of his daughter Gilda whom he carefully shields from the world.

In the street before Rigoletto's closely guarded house the hired assassin Sparafucile asks the jester for work. Rigoletto says he will send for him when the need arises. Inside the garden wall Rigoletto fondly greets his daughter Gilda. She fails to tell her father that she has met a handsome young student. After Rigoletto has departed the student enters the garden. It is the Duke in disguise, and the young couple exchange romantic vows. A group of nobles come into the street after the Duke has gone. They are all masked. When Rigoletto questions them they tell him they are about to kidnap a woman who interests the Duke. Rigoletto, his face covered by a mask, joins the fun. It is only after he has helped them abduct his own daughter that he realizes the horrible truth.

The Duke and Gilda are closeted together in the palace when Rigoletto enters, casually feigning indifference. Enraged by the mocking courtiers, he denounces them as a vile rabble. When Gilda enters and embraces her father the dumbfounded courtiers retire. Gilda tells Rigoletto what has passed between herself and the Duke. Rigoletto, recalling Monterone's curse, determines that it shall fall heavily on the Duke.

Rigoletto hires Sparafucile to murder the Duke at a lonely inn where the Duke is making love to Sparafucile's sister, and deliver his body in a sack at midnight. Sparafucile's sister pleads for the Duke's life and Sparafucile relents. If a substitute can be found for the sack the Duke's life will be spared. Gilda overhears the conversation and determines to sacrifice herself for the man she loves. When Rigoletto returns at midnight, it is to claim the body of his own murdered daughter. The curse is complete.

NOTES: WORLD PREMIERE: Fenice Theatre, Venice, Italy, March 11, 1851. *Cast:* Rigoletto, Felice Varesi; Duke of Mantua, Raffaele Mirate; Sparafucile, Pons; Maddalena, Casaloni; Gilda, Teresa Brambilla. AMERICAN PREMIERE: Academy of Music, New York City, February 19, 1855. *Cast:* Rigoletto, Ettore Barili; Duke of Mantua, Biagio Bolcioni; Sparafucile, Luigi Rocco; Maddalena, Amalia Patti-Strakosch; Gilda, Bertucca Maretzek. METROPOLITAN OPERA PREMIERE: November 16, 1883. *Cast:* Rigoletto, Luigi Guadagnini; Duke of Mantua, Roberto Stagno; Sparafucile, Franco Novara; Maddalena, Sofia Scalchi; Gilda, Marcella Sembrich.

Gilda begs her father's confidence

Rigoletto demands his daughter's release

Rigoletto shows Gilda the Duke's flirtation with Maddalena

ico Caruso who made his Met debut as The
ke, November 24, 1903

Titta Ruffo as Rigoletto

Giuseppe De Luca as Rigoletto

Ralph Errolle as The Duke

Marion Talley, who made her Met debut as Gilda, February 17, 1926, at the age of nineteen

Frieda Hempel as Gilda

Jan Kiepura as The Duke

Maria Barrientos as Gilda

Leonard Warren as Rigoletto

Sophie Braslau as Maddalena

Florencio Constantino
as The Duke

Ferruccio Tagliavini
as The Duke

Jan Peerce
as The Duke

Lawrence Tibbett
as Rigoletto

Eugene Conley as The Duke

Beniamino Gigli as The Duke

Mario Sammarco as Rigoletto

Jussi Bjoerling as The Duke　　[202]

Hilde Gueden as Gilda

Charles Kullman as The Duke

Tito Schipa as The Duke

Lily Pons and Nino Martini taking curtain calls at the Met performance of "Rigoletto," December 28, 1933, when Martini made his debut

Armand Tokatyan as The Duke

Amelita Galli-Curci made her American debut as Gilda, November 18, 1916, at the Auditorium, Chicago

Alessandro Bonci made his Met debut as The Duke, November 22, 1907

Titta Ruffi

John Charles Thomas as Rigoletto

Jean Madeira as Maddalena

Romeo and Juliette

BY CHARLES GOUNOD
Libretto by Jules Barbier and Michel Carré

Verona, the Middle Ages. At a masked ball Capulet introduces his daughter Juliette to society. Romeo, son of the rival Montague family, comes to the party masked and is at once struck by Juliette's beauty. Their meeting is cut short by Juliette's hot-tempered cousin Tybalt, who recognizes Romeo and threatens to kill him. Capulet, not wanting the festivities interrupted, permits Romeo to depart in peace as the ball continues.

In Capulet's garden Romeo risks danger for another glimpse of Juliette. She appears on her balcony and together they swear eternal faithfulness.

Romeo and Juliette come to Friar Laurence's cell to be secretly married. Hoping thus to end the hostility between the rival houses the friar consents to unite them.

In a street before Capulet's house Romeo's servant gets into a fight with a servant of the Capulet household. The fight quickly spreads to include Mercutio, Romeo's close friend, and Juliette's cousin Tybalt. Mercutio is wounded, and the enraged Romeo slays Tybalt. The Duke of Verona banishes Romeo for his part in the brawl.

Romeo and his bride take a last secret farewell before Capulet enters to insist that his daughter marry his kinsman Paris. Alone with Juliette, Friar Laurence suggests a plan whereby she may be reunited with Romeo. He gives her a sleeping potion which she is to drink before the wedding. It will place her in a death-like trance for two days, at the end of which time she may escape from her tomb and fly to Romeo. Capulet arrives with Paris, and Juliette, having drunk the potion, passes into a coma so deep that all think she is dead.

In the tomb Juliette lies on her bier. Romeo has heard of her supposed death and bursts into the chamber. Seeing his dead bride, the unhappy Romeo drinks poison. Juliette regains consciousness, and they embrace passionately before the poison takes effect. With Romeo dead, Juliette draws his dagger and stabs herself, and the lovers die in each other's arms.

Romeo meets Juliette at Capulet's Ball

Tybalt (Hardy Williams) is slain by Romeo (Orville Harrold) and Mercutio (Thomas Chalmers) is wounded

The young lovers are married by Friar Lawrence

Juliette's chamber

Bidu Sayao as Juliette with Jussi Bjöerling as Romeo

Juliette's bier in the tomb of the Capulets

Lois Ewell and Orville Harrold as Juliette and Romeo

NOTES: WORLD PREMIERE: Theatre Lyrique, Paris, France, April 27, 1867. *Cast:* Juliette, Caroline Miolan-Carvalho; Stephano, Daram; Gertrude, Duclos; Romeo, Michot; Tybalt, Puget; Mercutio, Barre; Paris, Laveissiere; Friar Laurence, Cazaux. AMERICAN PREMIERE (in Italian): Academy of Music, New York City, November 15, 1867. *Cast:* Juliette, Minnie Hauk; Stephano, Ronconi; Gertrude, Fleury; Romeo, Pancani; Tybalt, Testa; Mercutio, Dominico Orlandini; Friar Laurence, Medini. METROPOLITAN OPERA PREMIERE (in French): December 14, 1891. *Cast:* Juliette, Emma Eames; Romeo, Jean de Reszke; Tybalt, Victor Capoul; Stephano, Jane de Vigne; Gertrude, Mathilde Bauermeister; Mercutio, Jean Martapoura; Friar Laurence, Edouard de Reszke. This was first sung at the Metropolitan Opera House in Italian under Abbey and Grau, April 14, 1890, a supplementary spring season.

Adelina Patti

Nellie Melba

Famous
Juliettes

Emma Eames

Geraldine Farrar made
her Met debut as
Juliette, November 26,
1906

Lucrezia Bori

Marcella Sembrich

Amelita Galli-Curci

Grace Moore

[209]

Charles Hackett as Romeo

Edouard de Reszke made his Met debut as Friar
Lawrence, December 14, 1891

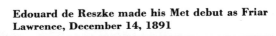

Riccardo Martin
as Romeo

Martial Singher
as Mercutio

Florencio Constantino
as Romeo

Josephine Jacoby as Stefano (1906)

Jean de Reszk
Romeo at his Met
December 14,

Edith Mason
as Juliette

Der Rosenkavalier

BY RICHARD STRAUSS
Libretto by Hugo Von Hofmannsthal

Vienna, during the reign of Maria Theresa. In her boudoir the youth Octavian declares his love for the Princess Von Werdenberg, with whom he has been having an affair. They are interrupted by sounds from without, and Octavian hides behind a screen, presently returning dressed as the Princess' maid. It is Baron Ochs at the door, the odious and boastful cousin of the Princess. He has come to ask her help in his approaching marriage with Sophie Faninal, and wishes her to recommend a gentleman to convey to his prospective bride the customary love-token, a silver rose. Seeing Octavian dressed as a girl he flirts outrageously. The Princess continues her morning levee, and the room is filled with hairdressers, a flute player, milliners, an Italian tenor and many others. The Princess agrees to arrange for the delivery of his Rose and the Baron departs. After a love scene with Octavian the Princess muses sadly that soon her charms will have faded and her lover gone.

In Faninal's house Octavian appears dressed in shimmering silver with the beautiful rose, but becoming enchanted with the lovely Sophie presses his own suit instead of the Baron's. When Ochs arrives Sophie is already in love with Octavian. In a comic duel Octavian lightly wounds the Baron on the hand. He sits moaning on the couch, and presently someone hands him a note from the Princess' 'ladies maid,' Octavian in disguise. Will not the Baron sup with her that night? The Baron anticipates a pleasant evening with the cute little maid.

In a tavern the disguised Octavian and the Baron sit at supper. Octavian has prearranged a host of tricks which confuse Ochs. Faces appear at windows, there are strange sounds, a woman enters with a horde of children claiming him as husband and father, and eventually even the police arrive. The confusion is quieted with the coming of the Princess. Octavian reveals his true nature to the flabbergasted Ochs who departs in haste. The melancholy Princess is resigned over the loss of her lover and unites Sophie and Octavian, who go off in a dream-like happiness.

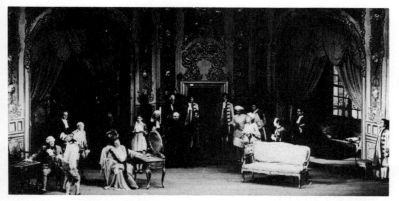

The Princess receives at her morning levee

Octavian (Jarmila Novotna)
declares his love for the Princess
(Lotte Lehmann)

Margarete Ober as Octavian with
Frieda Hempel as the Princess

Octavian presents the rose to Sophie

NOTES: WORLD PREMIERE: Royal Opera House, Dresden, Germany, January 26, 1911. *Cast:* Princess von Werdenberg, Margarete Siems; Baron Ochs, Karl Peron; Octavian, Eva von der Osten; Faninal, K. Scheidemontel; Sophie, Minnie Nast; Marianne, Riza Eibenschuetz; Valzacchi, Ruediger. AMERICAN PREMIERE: Metropolitan Opera House, New York City, December 9, 1913. *Cast:* Princess von Werdenberg, Frieda Hempel; Baron Ochs, Otto Goritz; Octavian, Margarete Ober; Faninal, Hermann Weil; Sophie, Anna Case; Singer, Carl Jorn.

Emanuel List as Baron Ochs

Risë Stevens as Octavian

Hilde Gueden as Sophie

Margarete Ober as Octavian with Anna Case as Sophie

**Florence Easton
as the Princess**

Otto Goritz as Baron Ochs

Frieda Hempel created the role of Princess von Werdenberg at
the American premiere

Maria Jeritza
with Marie Sundelius

**Marie Sundelius as Sophie with
Paul Bender as Baron Ochs**

Alexander Kipnis as Baron Ochs

Lotte Lehmann as the Princess

Jarmila Novotna as Octavian

Maria Jeritza as Octavian

Margarete Ober as Octavian

Kurt Baum as the Italian Singer

Salome

BY RICHARD STRAUSS
Libretto by Hedwig Lachmann

On a spacious terrace before Herod's palace stands a cistern in which Jokanaan the Prophet is imprisoned for his teachings. Herod hesitates to condemn the Prophet to death because he fears the vengeance of the Jews. Inside the palace a great banquet is being given by Herod and his wife Herodias. To escape the lecherous eye of her mother's husband Herod, the beautiful Salome comes out onto the terrace where she hears the compelling voice of Jokanaan coming from the cistern. At her insistence the Prophet is brought forth and he denounces the wicked and sinful Queen Herodias. Salome is greatly moved by the impressive man and longs to possess him. In her wild raving she desires to kiss his lips. The Prophet scorns her and descends once more into the well, while Salome, wild with passion, writhes on the gratings above.

The court come onto the terrace where the drunken Herod looks longingly at Salome. When the warning voice of the Prophet is again heard, Herod is urged to execute him, but still he hesitates. Fascinated by Salome, Herod begs her to dance before him, promising her anything if she will. She begins to dance in a wild orgy of frenzy. One by one she discards her veils. After the dance is completed the degenerate woman demands her reward. Urged on by her wicked mother she insists on having the head of the man who scorned her, Jokanaan. Such a terrible request shocks Herod and he begs her to desist. But Salome is firm. Nothing but the head of the Prophet will satisfy her. Into the well the executioners descend, emerging soon with the head of Jokanaan on a platter. The horrified people recoil, but the passionate Salome accepts the plate and begins a wild dance around and around the head. In the darkening night Salome dances in fascination, smothering the dead lips with her kisses. In revulsion and horror Herod orders his guards to kill her. The unholy degenerate is crushed to death under the heavy shields of the soldiers.

NOTES: WORLD PREMIERE: Dresden Royal Opera, Dresden, Germany, December 9, 1905. *Cast:* Salome, Marie Wittich; Herodias, Irene Chavanne; Herod, Carl Burrian; Jokanaan, Karl Perron; Narraboth, Jager; First Nazarene, Blaschke. AMERICAN PREMIERE: Metropolitan Opera House, New York City, January 22, 1907. *Cast:* Salome, Olive Fremstad; Herodias, Marion Weed; Herod, Carl Burrian; Jokanaan, Anton van Roy; Narraboth, Andreas Dippel; First Nazarene, Marcel Journet.

**Kerstin Thorborg
as Queen Herodias**

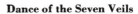

Dance of the Seven Veils

Phyllis Curtin, Frances Bible, Jim Hawthorne, Walter Cassell
of New York City Opera Company

Olive Fremstad sang Salome at the American premiere

Rene Maison as Herod

Salome watches Jokanaan in his imprisonment

Mary Garden as Salome

Emmy Destinn
as Salome

Mary Garden as Salome
with Charles Dalmores
as Herod

**Brian Sullivan
as Narraboth**

**Ljuba Welitch
as Salome**

Ljuba Welitch

**Hector Dufranne
as Jokanaan**

**Even Herod's court is shocked by
Salome's shameless exaltation**

Samson et Dalila

BY CAMILLE SAINT-SAËNS
Libretto by Ferdinand Lemaire

In ancient times the Hebrews languish in servitude to the Philistines. The mighty Samson urges them to trust in God and not give up hope. In a struggle with the Philistines Samson slays the Satrap of Gaza, which acts as a signal for a revolt of the Hebrews. Everywhere the Philistines flee, and their high priest curses Samson. From the temple comes the seductively beautiful Dalila surrounded by her priestesses. Despite his efforts to resist temptation, Samson is soon fascinated by the captivating woman. She invites him to come to her home in the Valley of Sorek. The mighty Samson wavers.

In her home Dalila calls on the powers of love to aid her in subduing Samson and bringing about his downfall. The high priest demands that she remain inflexible and find some way to deliver him up to the Philistines. Samson arrives to keep his rendezvous, and is soon greatly tempted by the seductress, who cautiously seeks the secret of his supernatural strength. At length Samson confesses that his strength lies in his hair. In her bedchamber he

falls asleep, and Dalila cuts off his long locks. The Philistines rush in and easily overpower him.

The helpless and blinded Samson is forced to turn the millstone which grinds corn for the Philistines. In his dark misery he beseeches the Lord for mercy, while from outside he hears the bitter retorts of his enslaved people, who reproach him for his weakness with Dalila.

The Philistines lead Samson away in triumph to their temple, where Dalila and her priestesses taunt him derisively, rejoicing over his downfall. Meanwhile Samson prays to his God. A small boy leads him to a spot between two massive marble pillars which support the entire roof of the temple. After a final prayer he feels his mighty strength returning. He grasps the two pillars, and in a tremendous effort, while all the others are lost in worship, the temple roof crashes down. The wicked Philistines and Samson are buried together.

NOTES: WORLD PREMIERE: Hoftheater, Weimar, Germany, Dec. 2, 1877. *Cast:* Samson, Ferenczy; High Priest, Milde; Dalila, Muller. AMERICAN PREMIERE: French Opera Company, New Orleans, La., January 4, 1893. *Cast:* Samson, Reynaud; High Priest, Chavreau; Dalila, Mounier; Abimelech, Hourdin. METROPOLITAN OPERA PREMIERE: February 8, 1895. *Cast:* Samson, Francesco Tamagno; Abimelech, Pol Plancon; High Priest, Giuseppe Campanari; Dalila, Augenia Mantelli.

An old Hebrew warns Samson
against the charms of Dalila

Seduction scene with Maria Gay
and Giovanni Zenatello

Enrico Caruso as Samson
chained to a mill

Ramon Vinay as Samson grips the pillars and prays
for strength to destroy the pagan rabble

Margarete Matzenauer as the wily Dalila

**Charles Dalmores
as Samson**

o Caruso
mson

Jeanne Gerville-Reache,
French contralto and
a popular Dalila,
made American debut
at Manhattan
Opera House in 1907

ud Wettergren,
'sh contralto,
lila

**Cyrena Van Gordon
as Dalila**

**Kathleen Howard
as Dalila**

Rise Stevens
as Dalila

Marguerite D'Alvarez
as Dalila

Rene Maison,
Belgian tenor
as Samson

Blanche Thebom
as Dalila

Carolina Lazzari
as Dalila

Enrico C

Siegfried

MUSIC AND LIBRETTO BY RICHARD WAGNER

In a smithy deep in the forest the Nibelung dwarf Mime tries to mend the broken pieces of the sword given to Siegfried by his mother Sieglinde into a weapon with which Siegfried can slay the giant Fafner, now in the form of a dragon, and regain the magic ring. But the sword refuses to weld. The God Wotan, disguised as a wanderer, comes to tell Mime that only he who knows no fear can forge the sword. When Siegfried returns from the forest Mime attempts to make him understand fear. Siegfried remains fearless, and when Mime tells him of the hideous dragon Fafner, the hero eagerly prepares to battle him. Seizing the broken fragments of the sword he forges them himself. Knowing that whoever kills Fafner and takes the ring will rule the world, Mime decides to murder Siegfried.

At the entrance to his cave the dragon Fafner awaits Siegfried, who joyously begins the battle and slays him quickly. A taste of the dragon's blood enables Siegfried to understand the language of the birds, who tell him to enter the cave and find the ring. With the ring in his possession he is able to read Mime's treacherous mind, and kills him forthwith. The birds direct him to the spot where Brunnhilde sleeps, encircled by the magic ring of fire.

In a wild mountainous spot Wotan tells Erda that he is willing to have Siegfried rule the world, but first his courage must be tested. When Siegfried comes seeking Brunnhilde Wotan blocks his path. Siegfried shatters Wotan's sword and plunges through the ring of fire to the sleeping Valkyrie. She greets him as the hero who will save the world and, discovering for the first time that she is a woman, sinks joyously into his ardent embrace.

NOTES: WORLD PREMIERE: Festival Theatre, Bayreuth, Germany, August 16, 1876. *Cast:* Wanderer, Franz Betz; Siegfried, Georg Unger; Alberich, Karl Hill; Mime, Karl Schlosser; Fafner, Franz von Reichenberg; Brunnhilde, Amalia Materna; Erda, Luise Jaïde; Forest Bird, Marie Haupt. AMERICAN PREMIERE: Metropolitan Opera House, New York City, November 9, 1887. *Cast:* Siegfried, Max Alvary; Mime, T. Ferenczy; Wanderer, Emil Fischer; Alberich, Rudolph von Milde; Fafner, Johannes Elmblad; Erda, Marianne Brandt; Brunnhilde, Lilli Lehmann; Forest Bird, Auguste Seidl-Kraus.

Siegfried confronts the dragon

Heinrich Hensel as Siegfried

Max Alvary as Siegfried

George Anthes as Siegfried

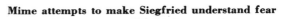

Mime attempts to make Siegfried understand fear

Lauritz Melchior
as Siegfried

Anton Van Rooy as Wotan

Heinrich Knote as Siegfried

Friedrich Schorr as Wotan

Set Svanholm as Siegfried

Jean de Reszke as Siegfried

Ernst Kraus as Siegfried

Andreas Dippel
as Siegfried

[231]

Simon recogn
his daughter

Simon Boccanegra

BY GIUSEPPE VERDI
Libretto by Francesco Maria Piave and Arrigo Boïto

Fourteenth century Genoa is torn by factions. The conspirator Paolo offers Simon Boccanegra the crown of the Doges, to thwart the hated aristocrat Fiesco. Boccanegra loves Fiesco's daughter, and joins the plot in hopes of obtaining her. Fiesco suddenly appears on his balcony to announce the death of his daughter. On seeing Boccanegra he becomes livid with rage. Boccanegra is the father of his daughter's illegitimate child.

Twenty-five years later Boccanegra rules as a tyrannical Doge. Fiesco, out of favor, secretly plots against Boccanegra. Living with him is Amelia, Boccanegra's daughter, and thus his own granddaughter, though neither she nor he knows it. Her lover Adorno has joined Fiesco's plot against the Doge. Their meeting is interrupted when the Doge himself appears to claim Amelia's hand as a reward for his henchman Paolo. Confessing that she is not Fiesco's daughter, Amelia shows the Doge a locket which convinces him she is his own child.

When Paolo learns that he cannot have Amelia after all, ʰe turns his anger on the Doge, and plots to abduct Amelia. Finding her gone, her frantic lover Adorno threatens to kill Boccanegra, whom he suspects, but is restrained when Amelia suddenly returns.

Paolo poisons Boccanegra's wine and the Doge unsuspectingly drinks. When Adorno learns the facts of Amelia's birth he humbly swears to help Boccanegra fight his enemies, giving up his alliance with Fiesco.

Fiesco's rebellion thus collapses, and Boccanegra generously pardons the leaders. Paolo whispers to Fiesco that he may still have his revenge, as the Doge will soon die of poison. In a death agony the Doge staggers to his throne. In his last moments he blesses the union of Amelia and Adorno, and tells his child that Fiesco is her own grandfather, hoping thus to put an end to the ancient feud.

NOTES: WORLD PREMIERE: Teatro Fenice, Venice, Italy, March 12, 1857. *Cast:* Paolo, Vercellini; Simon, Giraldoni; Fiesco, Eduverria; Amelia, Bendazzi; Gabriele, Negrini. REVISED OPERA PREMIERE: La Scala, Milan, Italy, March 24, 1881. *Cast:* Simon, Victor Maurel; Fiesco, Edouard de Reszke; Gabriele, Francesco Tamagno. AMERICAN PREMIERE: Metropolitan Opera House, January 28, 1932. *Cast:* Simon Boccanegra, Lawrence Tibbett; Fiesco, Ezio Pinza; Amelia, Marie Muller; Gabriele, Giovanni Martinelli.

**Giovanni Martinelli, the first to
sing Gabriele in America**

Amelia shows the Doge a locket, which convinces him she is his child

Simon blesses the union of Amelia and Adorno as he dies

Richard Tucker
as Gabriele

Astrid Varnay
as Amelia

Lawrence Tibbett who
sang the title role at the
American premiere

Hoffmann tells of his three strange infatuations

The Tales of Hoffmann

BY JACQUES OFFENBACH
Libretto by Jules Barbier and Michel Carré

At an inn his fellow students accuse Hoffmann of being in love. Denying the fact, he agrees to tell the story of his three strange infatuations.

The mechanical genius Coppelius has constructed a remarkable life-like doll which he sells to Spalanzani who introduces the doll to Hoffmann as his daughter Olympia. The evil Coppelius gives Hoffmann a pair of magic glasses with which he falls in love with the beautiful doll. The madly infatuated Hoffmann is spellbound as he watches Olympia sing and dance, until suddenly the enraged Coppelius smashes the doll in a hundred pieces. Spalanzani had attempted to pay for his creation with a worthless check, and Hoffmann's first love ends in disillusionment.

In Venice the beautiful courtesan Giulietta next attracts Hoffmann. The evil Dapertutto owns the soul of Schlemil, another of Giulietta's lovers, and hopes to get Hoffmann's soul too. Giulietta tells Hoffmann he may have the key to her bedroom if he challenges Schlemil for it. In a duel Hoffmann kills Schlemil, but instead of winning the courtesan he sees her passing in her gondola with Dapertutto, singing a mocking song at Hoffmann's expense.

In Germany Hoffmann has fallen in love with the deli-cately beautiful Antonia, whose dead mother was once a great singer. Antonia, too, has a beautiful voice but has been warned that singing will severely tax her fragile health. Miracle, the evil doctor who has haunted Hoffmann as Coppelius and Dapertutto, urges Antonia to sing. When she does the strain proves too great and she dies in Hoffmann's arms. His third love ends in tragedy.

Hoffmann has had three loves, one stemming from beauty, one from motives of passion, and one based on purer ideals. Now, only the muse of art will console him. She at least can never prove unfaithful. Hoffmann falls asleep back at the inn.

NOTES: WORLD PREMIERE: Opera Comique, Paris, France, February 10, 1881. *Cast:* Hoffmann, Talazac; Lindorf, Coppelius, Dr. Miracle, Emile Alex Taskin; Olympia, Adele Isaac; Antonia, Adele Isaac. AMERICAN PREMIERE: Fifth Avenue Theatre, New York City, October 16, 1882. *Cast:* Hoffmann, Maire; Lindorf, Mauge; Olympia, Derivis; Antonia, Anais Privot. METROPOLITAN OPERA PREMIERE: By Chicago-Philadelphia Opera Company, February 14, 1911. *Cast:* Hoffmann, Charles Dalmores; Lindorf, Armand Crabbe; Coppelius, Dappertutto and Dr. Miracle, Maurice Renaud; Olympia, Alice Zeppilli; Giulietta and Antonia, Margarita Sylva.

Spalanzani's Salon where Hoffmann meets Olympia

In Venice, Hoffmann falls in love with Giulietta

Hoffmann (Umberto Macnez) falls in love with Antonia (Lucrezia Bori)

Antonia dies. (L-R) Umberto Macnez, Lucrezia Bori, Leon Rothier, Giulio Rossi

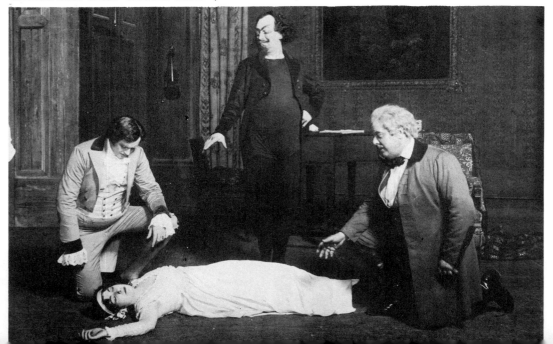

Charles Dalmores
as Hoffman

Lucrezia Bori as Giulietta

Johannes Sembach
as Hoffmann

Marcella Semb

Alice Zeppilli who sang Olympia at
the Metropolitan premiere

Edmond Clément
as Hoffmann

Nicola Moscona
as Crespel

The song contest

Elisabeth rescues Tannhauser from the indignant knights

Tannhauser

MUSIC AND LIBRETTO BY RICHARD WAGNER

In the thirteenth century the Knight Tannhauser has grown tired of the alluring attractions of Venus and longs to return to Thuringia. Angrily Venus orders him to depart, but warns him that he will soon wish he were back. Suddenly Tannhauser finds himself in a beautiful valley. The Venusberg and its seductive mistress have miraculously disappeared. A group of pilgrims bound for Rome pass. Tannhauser kneels in prayer but is interrupted by the appearance of the Landgrave of Thuringia and a party of hunters. The knights, recognizing him as a lost brother who suddenly departed when he was unsuccessful in a song contest, welcome Tannhauser back to their company. They depart for the nearby Wartberg where Tannhauser agrees to enter another song contest. His friend Wolfram tells him that his singing in the previous contest won the heart of Elizabeth, the Landgrave's niece.

Elizabeth is happy over Tannhauser's return and greets him warmly. Wolfram, himself in love with Elizabeth, is the first to sing in the contest, a song extolling pure and heavenly love. When Tannhauser answers with a passionate avowal of the pagan joys of sensuous love, the company are aghast. The insulted knights draw their swords but Elizabeth begs for Tannhauser's life. The sound of pilgrims is heard in the distance, and Tannhauser joins them to seek forgiveness from the Pope at Rome.

Elizabeth has heard nothing of the blasphemous Tannhauser. Her prayers remain unanswered. Wolfram sadly concludes that the unhappy Elizabeth will soon be in heaven. Tannhauser stumbles into the valley, ragged and dishevelled. The Pope has refused pardon, saying he will not be forgiven until the Pope's staff sprouts leaves. The desperate knight longs for the Venusberg, but news comes that Elizabeth is dead, and Tannhauser collapses in remorse. Pilgrims arrive with the Pope's staff. It has miraculously sprouted leaves, and Tannhauser has been forgiven.

NOTES: WORLD PREMIERE: Royal Opera House, Dresden, Germany, October 19, 1845. *Cast:* Tannhauser, Joseph Aloys Tichatschek; Venus, Wilhelmine Schroder-Devrient; Walther, Schloss; Wolfram von Eschenbach, Metterwurzer; Elizabeth, Johanna Wagner (composer's niece). AMERICAN PREMIERE: Stadt Theatre, New York City, April 4, 1859. *Cast:* Tannhauser, Hugo Pickaneser; Venus, Frau Pickaneser; Walther, Lotti; Wolfram von Eschenbach, Lehmann; Elizabeth, Sidenburg. METROPOLITAN OPERA PREMIERE: November 17, 1884. *Cast:* Tannhauser, Anton Schott; Venus, Anna Slach; Walther, Emil Tiferro; Wolfram von Eschenbach, Adolf Robinson; Elizabeth, Auguste Seidl-Kraus.

Wolfram overhears Elisabeth's prayer

Lilli Lehmann
as Venus

Emma Eames as Elisabeth

Albert Niemann as Tannhauser

Marjorie Lawrence with Lauritz Melchior

[239]

Lawrence Tibbett as Wolfram

Alexander Kipnis as the Landgrave

Geraldine Farrar
as Elisabeth

uise Homer as Venus

Ernst Kraus as Tannhauser

Milka Ternina as Elisabeth

Helen Traubel
as Elisabeth

[241]

Margaret Harshaw as Venus

John Garris as Walther

Marcel Journet as the Landgrave

Kirsten Flagstad
as Elisabeth

Cyrena Van Gordon as Venus

Olive Fremstad as Venus

Marcella Sembrich as Elisabeth

Herbert Janssen as Wolfram

Ernst Van Dyck as Tannhauser

Martial Singher as Wolfram

Johanna Gadski as Elisabeth

Nellie Melba as Elisabeth

Mauritz Melchior made his Met debut as Tannhauser, February 17, 1926

Maria Jeritza
as Elisabeth

Rosa Raisa as Elisabeth

Thais

BY JULES MASSENET
Libretto by Louis Gallet

In the early Christian era the voluptuous Thais symbolizes the corruption and luxury of Alexandria. The Cenobite monk Athanael is determined to convert Thais to his faith and turn the wicked city away from sin. In a dream he sees Thais naked in the theatre, applauded by the people as Aphrodite. Bent on reform, despite the protests of his fellow monks, Athanael sets out for Alexandria.

At the home of his friend Nicias, Athanael finds that Thais has infatuated Nicias. Nevertheless, when the skeptical Nicias hears Athanael's purpose he agrees to help. At a great banquet Athanael meets Thais, who is curious about the strange monk. Learning his purpose she deliberately shocks him by posing as Aphrodite and Athanael leaves horrified.

After a night of debauchery Thais returns alone to her home. Athanael comes to her there telling her the love he offers is from God. Thais attempts to seduce him but fails, and Athanael departs, saying he will wait for Thais outside her house.

Thais comes to the waiting Athanael prepared to give up her worldly goods, devote her life to God, and enter a convent. Destroying all traces of her sinful life, Athanael and Thais set fire to her palace. A crowd of revelers are enraged to find Thais leaving them, and attempt to kill Athanael, but are prevented by Nicias. Thais and the monk start off into the desert.

Entrusting Thais to the nuns Athanael bids her farewell. But unable to think of anything but her intoxicating beauty Athanael confesses that he has saved her soul at the cost of his own. Unable to remain away he begs Thais to return to him and earthly love. The worn and repentent Thais does not heed him, and dying, sings of the gates of heaven opening for her.

Pasquale Amato with Geraldine Farrar

Thais infatuates Nicias

A night of debauchery

Thais lies dying in a convent

**Armand Tokatyan
as Nicias**

NOTES: WORLD PREMIERE: Paris Opera House, Paris, France, March 16, 1894. *Cast:* Thais, Sibyl Sanderson; Athanael, Jean Francoise Delmas; Albine, Mme. Beauvais; Nicias, Albert Alvarez. AMERICAN PREMIERE: Manhattan Opera House, New York City, November 25, 1907. *Cast:* Thais, Mary Garden (American debut); Albine, Giuseppina Giaconia; Athanael, Maurice Renaud; Nicias, Charles Dalmores. METROPOLITAN OPERA PREMIERE: February 16, 1917. *Cast:* Thais, Geraldine Farrar; Nicias, Luca Botta; Athanael, Pasquale Amato; Albine, Kathleen Howard.

**Geraldine Farrar
as Thais**

**Clarence Whitehill
as Athanael**

Lina Cavalieri as Thais

Charles Dalmores
as Nicias

Maria Jeritza as Thais

José Mojica as Nicias

Cesare Formichi as Athanael

Mary Garden made her American debut as Thais, November 25, 1907, at Manhattan Opera House

Marguerite Namara
as Thais

Pasquale Amato
as Athanael

Tosca

BY GIACOMO PUCCINI
Libretto by Luigi Illica and Giuseppe Giac⟨

Scarpia in the church

Cavaradossi refuses to betray Angelotti to Scarpia

After the murder of Scarpia, Tosca places candlesticks at his head

Scarpia's soldiers prepare to execute Cavaradossi

NOTES: WORLD PREMIERE: Teatro Castanzi, Rome, Italy, January 14, 1900. *Cast:* Tosca, Heraclea Darclee; Cavaradossi, Emilio de Marchi; Scarpia, Eugenio Giraldoni. AMERICAN PREMIERE: Metropolitan Opera House, New York City, February 4, 1901. *Cast:* Tosca, Milka Ternina; Cavaradossi, Giuseppe Cremonini; Scarpia, Antonio Scotti.

Rome, 1800. In a church the artist Mario Cavaradossi is painting a Madonna which resembles the singer Tosca, whom he loves. The escaped political prisoner Angelotti rushes in seeking a hiding place and Mario hides him in the chapel. Tosca arrives and finds Mario ill at ease. She accuses him of infidelity but Mario reassures her. After she has gone Mario assists Angelotti to escape disguised as a woman. Baron Scarpia, the Chief of Police, enters seeking Angelotti. He finds a fan dropped by Angelotti and Mario is under suspicion of aiding the prisoner. Tosca returns and Scarpia's attention focuses on this beautiful woman he has long desired to possess. When he shows her the fan which Angelotti dropped Tosca believes Mario has been with another woman and her jealousy returns.

In his apartment Scarpia finishes dinner. Mario is being tortured to reveal Angelotti's hiding place when Tosca arrives. Hearing the screams of her lover she finally reveals Angelotti's secret. Mario is revived and, bitterly denouncing Tosca for informing, is dragged off to prison to await execution as an accomplice. Tosca begs for her lover's life. Scarpia agrees to free Mario if Tosca will submit to him. When she consents Scarpia explains there will have to be a mock execution, after which she and Mario can escape. He writes a passport allowing them to leave Rome. Approaching the desperate woman, he is stabbed with a table knife. Tosca snatches the passport from his fingers and hurriedly rushes out.

Tosca comes on the morning of Mario's execution to tell him of the plan. Mario prepares to go through with the mock ceremony. But Scarpia has the final revenge. His villainy is complete and the execution is genuine. Mario falls dead before the firing squad. As the soldiers, having found Scarpia's body, attempt to seize Tosca she leaps from the parapet to her death in the Tiber River.

**Pasquale Amato
as Scarpia**

**Maria Jeritza as Tosca which she sang for the first time
at the Met Dec. 1, 1921**

**Giovanni Martinelli made his American
debut in Philadelphia on Nov. 3, 1913,
as Cavaradossi**

Maurice Renaud
as Scarpia

Milka Ternina, first
Tosca at American
premiere, Met,
Feb. 4, 1901

Giovanni Zenatello
as Mario

**Lawrence Tibbett
as Scarpia**

**Giuseppe Cremonini, first
Cavaradossi in America. Sung at
Met, Feb. 4, 1901**

**Marjorie Lawrence
as Tosca**

**Rosa Raisa
as Tosca**

**Olive Fremstad
as Tosca**

**Geraldine Farrar made her first
appearance as Tosca at Met,
Nov. 22, 1909**

[253]

Lina Cavalieri, the most beautiful of all Toscas

Emma Eames as Tosca, the role of her
Metropolitan farewell, Feb. 15, 1909

Antonio Scotti in hi
most famous role
Scarpia, which he sang
at the American
premiere, Met Oper
House, Feb. 4, 190▶

Claudia Muzio made
her Met debut as Tosca,
Dec. 4, 1916

Mary Garden
as Tosca

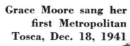

Grace Moore sang her
first Metropolitan
Tosca, Dec. 18, 1941

**Enrico Caruso
as Cavaradossi**

Jan Kiepura
as Cavaradossi

Mario Chamlee made debut at Met
as Cavaradossi, Nov. 22, 1920

**Emmy Destinn
as Tosca**

Charles Kullmann
as Cavaradossi

**Licia Albanese
as Tosca**

**Mario Del Monaco
as Cavaradossi**

**Elisabeth Rethberg
as Tosca**

Angelo Minghetti
as Cavaradossi

Beniamino Gigli
as Cavaradossi

George London
as Scarpia

Jan Peerce
as Cavaradossi

Lotte Lehmann
as Tosca

La Traviata

BY GIUSEPPE VERDI
Libretto by Francesco Maria Piave

Paris in 1700. In the elaborate drawing room of the courtesan Violetta a party is in progress. Already ill with consumption Violetta nevertheless insists on gaiety. She is impressed with a rich young man named Alfredo Germont and when they are alone he confesses he is in love with her. Hesitantly Violetta returns his affection and, finding great happiness, determines to give up her life of pleasure. Together the lovers will find a new life of seclusion in the country far from sinful Paris.

After months of happiness in the country Alfredo discovers that Violetta is preparing to sell her property in order to meet their expenses. He leaves for Paris to raise some money. After he has gone his father Germont is announced. Discreetly he begs Violetta to give up his son. The scandal is threatening the happiness of his daughter. Violetta, desperate and unhappy, agrees to leave Alfredo

and prepares a letter of farewell. When he suddenly returns she pretends nothing has happened. After she has gone Alfredo finds the note and angrily prepares to follow her to Paris.

At a masked ball Violetta enters on the arm of a former lover. Alfredo finds her there and in a rage hurls money at her feet, asking everyone to witness that he is returning the money she spent on him. When his father enters and upbraids him he begins to understand that the sick Violetta still loves him.

Violetta lies in her bedroom desperately ill. The doctor tells her maid she has only a few hours to live. Violetta reads of Alfredo in a letter from his father. He is returning, having discovered her sacrifice. But it is already too late. They embrace passionately, and as Alfredo swears he will never leave her again, she sinks back in his arms dead.

Violetta (Licia Albanese) toasts her new friend
Alfredo (Eugene Conley)

Alfredo's father urges Violetta to leave him

NOTES: WORLD PREMIERE: Fenice Theatre, Venice, Italy, March 6,
1853. *Cast:* Alfredo, Lodovico Graziani; Germont, Felice Varesi;
Violetta, Fanny Salvini-Donatelli; Flora, Speranza. AMERICAN PRE-
MIERE: Academy of Music, New York City, December 3, 1856. *Cast:*
Alfredo, Pasquale Brignoli; Germont, Amodio; Baron Douphol,
Gasparoni; Violetta, Anna de LaGrange; Flora, Siedenburg. MET-
ROPOLITAN OPERA PREMIERE: November 5, 1883. *Cast:* Alfredo,
Victor Capoul; Germont, Giuseppe Del Puente; Baron Douphol,
Achille Augier; Violetta, Marcella Sembrich; Flora, Emily La-
blache.

Opening night
performance (Dec. 16,
1935) of Metropolitan
Opera Company
season with L. Bori
as Violetta, L. Tibbett
as Giorgio and
R. Crooks as Alfredo

Alfredo returns to the
dying Violetta

Frieda Hempel
as Violetta

Rosa Ponselle
as Violetta

FAMOUS VIOLETTAS

Jarmila Novotna
as Violetta

Claudia Muzio
as Violetta

**Anna de La Grange, first to
sing Violetta in America at Academy
of Music, N.Y.C., Dec. 3, 1856**

**Marcella Sembrich, first Violetta
at the Met on Nov. 5, 1883**

Licia Albanese

Helen Jepson

Nellie Melba

Lily Pons

FAMOUS VIOLETTAS

Lina Cavalieri

Geraldine Farrar

Frances Alda

Antonio Scotti
as Germont

Beniamino Gigli
as Alfredo

Richard Crooks
as Alfredo

John Charles Thomas
sang Germont in his
Met debut February 2,
1934

Giuseppe Di Stefano and
Bidu Sayao as Alfredo and Violetta

Leonard Warren
as Germont

Amelita Galli-Curci first sa
Violetta at the Auditori
Theatre with the Chicago Ope
Company, Dec. 1, 19
She made her Met debut in
same role, Nov. 14, 19

[262]

Tristan und Isolde

MUSIC AND LIBRETTO BY RICHARD WAGNER

In legendary times Tristan is bringing the Irish Princess Isolde in his ship to Cornwall, where she is to become the bride of King Marke. Hating Tristan for the murder of her lover, and unhappy by the thought of a loveless marriage, Isolde decides to poison herself and Tristan and commands her servant Brangaene to prepare a deadly drug. Not wanting to see her mistress dead Brangaene substitutes a love potion. When Tristan and Isolde drink, instead of the desired death, they gaze at each other in ecstasy, then sink into one another's arms as the sailors shout that the ship has arrived in Cornwall.

King Marke has gone on a hunting expedition and Isolde signals to Tristan. They meet rapturously by moonlight in the garden, oblivious to the warning of Brangaene, who tells Isolde that they are being watched by Melot, one of her husband King Marke's henchmen. Suddenly Tristan's faithful companion Kurvenal rushes in urging Tristan to save himself, but it is already too late. Melot and the King surprise the guilty lovers, and Tristan is bitterly reproached by the disappointed King. Melot draws his sword and attacks Tristan. In the battle Tristan receives a mortal wound.

In a courtyard of Tristan's castle in Brittany the wounded knight is being tended by his faithful retainer Kurvenal. Only Isolde's healing touch can save Tristan from death, and Kurvenal searches the seacoast for any sight of her ship. The delirious Tristan fancies she is coming but no ship is in sight. When Isolde finally approaches the excited knight feverishly tears off his bandages and attempts to rise up to meet her. It is too late, and Tristan falls back dead in Isolde's arms. King Marke follows with Melot. Thinking they have come to kill his master, Kurvenal attacks them and is killed. Unable to reunite the lovers as he had hoped to do, King Marke approaches to find Isolde dying of grief over Tristan's body.

NOTES: WORLD PREMIERE: Royal Court Theatre, Munich, Germany, June 10, 1865. *Cast:* Tristan, Ludwig Schnorr von Carolsfeld; Kurvenal, Mitterwurzer; Isolde, Malvina Schnorr von Carolsfeld; King Marke, Zottmoyer; Melot, Heinrich; Brangaene, Deinet. AMERICAN PREMIERE: Metropolitan Opera House, New York City, December 1, 1886. *Cast:* Tristan, Albert Niemann; King Marke, Emil Fischer; Isolde, Lilli Lehmann; Kurvenal, Adolf Robinson; Melot, Rudolph von Milde; Brangaene, Marianne Brandt.

The love potion

Lilli Lehmann created Isolde in America at the Met, December 1, 1886

Tristan brings Isolde to Cornwall in his ship

Melot and the King surprise the guilty lovers

Tristan falls dead in Isolde's arms

Herbert Janssen as Kurvenal

Milka Ternina

Helen Traubel sang her first Isolde
December 4, 1942

Isolde (Marjorie Lawrence)
commands Brangaene (Kerstin
Thorborg) to prepare a deadly
drug. Tristan (Lauritz Melchior)

Margarete Matzenauer
as Isolde

Ramon Vinay
as Tristan

Albert Niemann sang first
Tristan at American premiere

Johanna Gadski made her farewell appearance as Isolde, April 13, 1917

Olive Fremstad sang her first Isolde January 1, 1908

Lillian Nordica last sang Isolde at the Met December 8, 1909. First sang the role November 27, 1895

Kirsten Flagstad sang
her first Isolde
February 6, 1935

Jean de Reszke sang his first Tristan November 27, 1895

David Bispham as Kurvenal

Michael Bohnen as King Marke

Cyrena Van Gordon as Brangaene

Lauritz Melchior as Tristan

Alexander Kipnis as King Marke

Olive Fremstad
as Brangaene

Clotilde Bressler-Gianoli
as Brangaene

[271]

Il Trovatore

BY GIUSEPPE VERDI
Libretto by Salvatore Cammarano

In fifteenth century Spain a retainer of the Count di Luna tells of how the Count's brother, when an infant, was bewitched by a gypsy. The gypsy was burned at the stake and her daughter, Azucena, revenged her death by kidnapping the infant child.

In the palace gardens Leonora, who is loved by the Count himself, confesses to her attendant that the troubadour Manrico has infatuated her. When Manrico comes serenading beneath her window the Count stormily interrupts them. In a duel Manrico is wounded and the angry di Luna swears to have him killed.

Deep in the mountains the gypsies camp for the night. Azucena, having nursed Manrico well, tells him how the Count's father burned her mother and how in revenge she seized the child to throw into the flames. In her frenzy, however, she burned her own child, and Manrico, brother of Count di Luna, was spared. She has raised him as her own. News comes that Leonora, thinking Manrico is dead, is about to enter a convent.

In the convent courtyard di Luna and his followers prepare to abduct Leonora but are interrupted by Manrico. Together Leonora and Manrico flee.

Azucena is captured by the Count whose hatred grows when he learns she murdered his brother and is Manrico's mother. He determines to burn her at the stake.

When Manrico is told of his mother's capture he rushes off to save her.

Manrico has been defeated by the Count and languishes in prison with his mother. Leonora begs mercy of the Count and promises to marry him if he will free Manrico.

Zelia Trebelli, first Met Azucena

Manrico hears from Leonora the price of his freedom and angrily denounces her. But Leonora falls back dying. She has taken poison to cheat di Luna. The Count is enraged over her death and immediately executes Manrico. Azucena tells the Count he has killed his own brother. Her revenge is complete.

NOTES: WORLD PREMIERE: Apollo Theatre, Rome, Italy, January 19, 1853. *Cast:* Leonora, Penco; Azucena, Goggi; Inez, Quadri; Fernando, Balderi; Manrico, C. Baucardé. AMERICAN PREMIERE: Academy of Music, New York City, May 2, 1855. *Cast:* Leonora, Bina Steffanone; Azucena, Felicita Vestvali; Inez, Avogrado; Fernando, Rocco; Manrico, Pasquale Brignoli. METROPOLITAN OPERA PREMIERE: October 26, 1883. *Cast:* Leonora, Alwina Valleria; Azucena, Zelia Trebelli; Inez, Imogene Forti; Fernando, Achile Augier; Manrico, Roberto Stagno.

Leonora comes into her garden to meet Manrico but finds instead Count di Luna

Leonora's garden

Manrico rescues Leonora from di Luna in the Convent cloister

The Convent cloister

Count di Luna's followers capture Azucena

Leonora lies dying

**Riccardo Martin
as Manrico**

**Claudia Muzio
as Leonora**

Enrico Caruso as Manrico

Lucien Muratore as Manrico

Louise Homer as Azucena

Jerome Hines as Fernando

Schumann-Heink as Azucena

Joseph Schwartz as Count di Luna

Beniamino Gigli as Manrico

[275]

Sieglinde (Astrid Varnay) and
Siegmund (Set Svanholm)
rest after their flight, protected by
Brunhilde (Margaret Harshaw)

Die Walkure

MUSIC AND LIBRETTO BY RICHARD WAGNER

A mighty hero must be found to regain the magic ring from the giants who jealously guard it. Wotan hopes the child of Siegmund and Sieglinde will be that hero. But while they are still young the hunter Hunding carries off Sieglinde and leaves Siegmund alone in the world. Years later Siegmund comes to Hunding's hut where Sieglinde, not knowing who he is, gives him food. Hunding recognizes in Siegmund his mortal enemy. Siegmund is offered the hospitality of the hut for the night, but on the morrow Hunding intends to kill him in battle. At the evening meal Hunding is drugged by Sieglinde into a deep sleep. Sieglinde reveals to Siegmund the hilt of a sword buried in a tree which only a great hero may withdraw. With a mighty effort Siegmund pulls out the weapon. Recognizing her long lost brother, Sieglinde falls into his arms and together they flee into the night.

In the forest the God Wotan bids his daughter Brunn-hilde defend Siegmund against Hunding, but his wife Fricka insists Siegmund must be punished for his union with his sister Sieglinde. Sadly the God instructs his daughter to make sure Hunding is victorious but Brunn-hilde disobeys his command and aids Siegmund in battle with Hunding. Wotan is forced at the last moment to interfere and Siegmund is slain, while Brunnhilde carries Sieglinde away.

On a rocky summit Brunnhilde faces her angry father. Sieglinde has been sent deep into the forest where she will give birth to the hero Siegfried. Wotan punishes his disobedient daughter by placing her in a deep sleep, surrounded by a wall of fire, which may be penetrated only by a great hero. With a final glance at his favorite Val-kyrie, as she sleeps surrounded by the magic fire, Wotan sorrowfully departs through the flames.

Sieglinde and Hunding
with their guest
Siegmund

Wotan (Schorr) tells Brunnhilde
(Flagstad) of his woes

Helen Traubel
as Brunnhilde

NOTES: WORLD PREMIERE: Munich, Germany, June 26, 1870. *Cast:* Brünnhilde, Sophie Stehle; Fricka, Kaufmann; Sieglinde, Therese Thomas; Wotan, Adolf Kinderman; Hunding, Bausewein; Siegmund, Heinrich Vogl. AMERICAN PREMIERE: Academy of Music, New York City, April 2, 1877. *Cast:* Brünnhilde, Eugenie Pappenheim; Fricka, Listner; Sieglinde, Pauline Canissa; Siegmund, Alexander Bischoff; Wotan, Felix Preusser; Hunding, Alouin Blum. METROPOLITAN OPERA PREMIERE: January 30, 1885. *Cast:* Brünnhilde, Amalia Materna; Fricka, Marianne Brandt; Sieglinde, Auguste Kraus; Siegmund, Anton Schott; Wotan, Josef Staudigl; Hunding, Josef Kögel.

Frederick Schorr
as Wotan

Lauritz Melchior as Siegmund with
Kirsten Flagstad as Brunhilde

Margarete Matzenauer
as Brunnhilde

Johanna Gadski
as Brunnhilde

Anton Van Rooy made
his Met debut as
Wotan, December 14, 1898

Clarence Whitehill
as Wotan

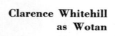

Kirsten Flagstad
made her Met debut
February 2, 1935,
singing Sieglinde

Cyrena Van Gordon
as Brunnhilde

Milka Ternina
as Brunnhilde

Astrid Varnay
who made her Met
debut singing Sieglinde,
December 6, 1941

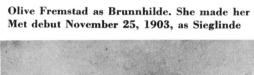

Olive Fremstad as Brunnhilde. She made her
Met debut November 25, 1903, as Sieglinde

Marie Olszewska
as Fricka

Maria Jeritza
as Sieglinde

Louise Homer
as Fricka

Paul Althouse
as Siegmund

Ernst Van Dyck
as Siegmund

Set Svanholm
as Siegmund

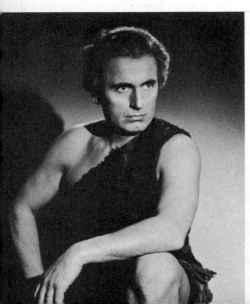

Johannes Sembach
as Siegmund

Lilli Lehmann
as Brunhilde

Rose Bampton
as Sieglinde

Lotte Lehmann
as Sieglinde

Elisabeth Rethberg
as Sieglinde

Berta Morena
as Sieglinde

Amalia Materna, first to sing
Brunnhilde at the Met,
January 30, 1887

[282]

Lauritz Melchior
as Siegmund

Kirsten Flagstad sang
her first Brunnhilde
at the Met
January 22, 1936

Marjorie Lawrence
made her debut at the
Met December 18,
1935, as Brunnhilde

Eugenie Pappenheim,
first American
Brunnhilde

Other Operas

Luigi Vellucci, Margery Mayer and David Poleri
of the New York City Center Opera Company

Beniamino Gigli
as Andrea Chenier

Rosa Ponselle
as Maddalena

Andrea Chenier

Umberto Giordano's opera *Andrea Chenier* is based o
the life of the remarkable poet and patriot of 18th Centur
France who was executed three days before the end of th
reign of terror during the French Revolution, 1794. I
cidents from Chenier's life are used in the opera, whic
appeared the year *La Boheme* had its world premier
1896, with Mario Sammarco singing a leading role. Gio
dano was an extraordinary genius of the verismo schoo
and this, his most popular opera, is a good vehicle fo
a dramatic soprano. It was performed 44 times in 1
seasons at the Metropolitan, and it was the object of
gala Hammerstein production in 1908, with Cleofont
Campanini conducting and his wife Eva Tetrazzini, siste
of Luisa, coming out of retirement to sing. A slipshod pr
duction in Boston in 1896 represented the first Americ
production. In 1921 the Metropolitan produced it for th
first time with Gigli as Chenier and Muzio in the role o
Maddalena.

Claudia Muzio and Giuseppe Danise sang at
the Metropolitan premiere, March 7, 1921

The Finale

Armand Tokatyan with Hilda Burke

The Bartered Bride

The most popular of all folk operas is Friedrich Smetana's colorful Czech work, *The Bartered Bride*. Smetana, creator of a national style in Czech music, wrote many operas but this remains his most enduring. At its world premiere in Prague, 1866, the dialogue was spoken. The swift pace, vivid and colorful music, and light-hearted gaiety of the score made it an instant success. It appeared in Vienna in 1893, and in America at the Haymarket Theatre, Chicago, the same year. Sixteen years later the Metropolitan put it on with Gustav Mahler in the pit, and Emmy Destinn singing the lead. A revival in 1926 featured Maria Muller, Bohnen, and Artur Bodanzky conducting. Rethberg was a later Maria. The opera was given an English production during a special spring season at the Metropolitan in 1936, and in the 1941 season Jarmila Novotna, another native of Czechoslovakia, had success in it.

George Gaynes
as Dandini

Riccardo Manning with Frances Bible

La Cenerentola

Arthur Manning, Frances Bible, Riccardo Manning and George Gayn...

Rossini's witty and delightful treatment of the Cinderella legend, *La Cenerentola,* was first performed in Rome in 1817. From that time until 1880, it was given every year with great success, but as styles changed, it was produced less frequently, though it remains his most popular work, after *The Barber of Seville.* It quickly became very popular in 19th Century America. Alboni made her American debut in the title role. The opera contains the most difficult vocal music Rossini wrote, requiring a mezzo voice with coloratura agility. Conchita Supervia was very successful in the role in our time, but the decline in florid singing prevents it from being heard often today, though there was a highly successful production at the New York City Center in the 1950's. *Cenerentola* was given at the Park Theatre in New York in 1825 by the Garcia Troupe, with Garcia's daughter Marie Malibran, who was seventeen at the time, creating a furore in the title role.

Ezio Pinza as King Dodon

Le Coq D'Or

Rimsky-Korsakoff had great trouble getting his panto-mime-opera *Le Coq d'Or* produced during his lifetime. The censors refused to allow a production, objecting to the implied criticism of Russian officialdom and bureaucracy, and it was not until after the composer died that it was first produced at Zimin's Private Theatre, Moscow, in 1910. The opera was taxing for singers obliged to dance as well, and over the protests of the Korsakoff family Fokine devised a plan whereby the singers sat at the side of the stage while dancers performed the action in the center. This mode was used successfully at Petrograd and became the standard form in Paris, London, and New York, where the American premiere took place at the Metropolitan in 1918. Marie Barrientos sang the Queen, and Adamo Didur appeared as King Dodon. The opera was given in French and Rosina Galli danced the Queen in the pantomime. Since that day it has been given over 50 times at the Met, with Breslau, Sundelius, Garrison, Galli-Curci, Talley, Pons, and Pinza among the famous singers taking part. Second only to *Boris* in popularity, this Russian opera contains much of Rimsky-Korsakoff's most fluent music, and is popular with coloratura sopranos who find it difficult to resist the shimmering "Hymn to the Sun".

Maurice Renaud as Mephistopheles

The Damnation of Faust

Hector Berlioz, the founder of program music, had a great influence on music in general, but none of his operas is well known on the stage of English-speaking countries. In its original form *The Damnation of Faust* was not an opera but a dramatic cantata, and as such it was first performed, in 1846. It was not until 1893, a quarter of a century after Berlioz' death, that it appeared as an opera in Monte Carlo, with Jean de Reszke as Faust. Melba and Calvé, Renaud and Alvarez sang it often in Europe. Though it had been done in its original form in New York in 1880, Leopold Damrosch conducting, it was not until 1906 that it appeared as an opera at the Metropolitan with Geraldine Farrar, who had made her local debut only two weeks before. Plançon was the Mephistopheles. It has not been given there since that season.

Dinorah

Meyerbeer's *Dinorah* occasionally appears as a vehicle for a soprano capable of executing its extraordinary coloratura music, but its inane and fatuous libretto, a treatment of an old Breton legend about a mad peasant girl, renders it unacceptable to modern audiences. Yet it does contain one famous aria, the Shadow Song, which made Galli-Curci's fortune, and sustained many another gifted soprano. Galli-Curci was so fond of the role they say she left the Chicago Opera because the managers refused to let her sing it as often as she wished. It was the role of her New York debut, in 1918. Despite a costly production for her at the Met, Galli-Curci sang it only twice there. First produced at the Opera Comique, Paris, in 1859, it appeared in America in 1864. Patti, Tetrazzini, and Marie Van Zandt also sang it successfully in this country.

Amelita Galli-Curci as Dinorah

**Lawrence Tibbett created the title role at the Met,
January 7, 1933**

The Emperor Jones

Russian-born Luis Gruenberg used Eugene O'Neill's
weirdly dramatic play about the thieving scoundrel Brutus
Jones who died by the silver bullet as the basis for the
very successful American opera *The Emperor Jones*. With
half-sung, half-spoken vocal effects, the opera created a
sensation at its premiere at the Metropolitan in 1933, and
Lawrence Tibbett in the title role gave what many considered his most effective creation. Tullio Serafin conducted this performance, which was given in double bill
with *Pagliacci*. It had ten repetitions in two seasons
and has been unheard since. The opera had been scheduled
for production in Berlin but was dropped, perhaps because an American opera dealing with negroes would
prove unacceptable to the Germany of nascent Naziism.

Ernani

Victor Hugo's famous play Hernani provided Sarah Bernhardt with one of her most effective roles. It also provid[ed] the early Verdi with a good idea for an opera, and *Erna[ni]* is the earliest of Verdi's works still occasionally produc[ed]. Its world premiere was at the Fenice Theatre, Venice, [in] 1844. London saw it in 1845, and New York in 1846. [It] took longer to reach Paris because Victor Hugo rais[ed] objections, and the characters had to be changed to It[al]ians. *Ernani* was the first grand opera ever given in S[an] Francisco, in 1853, and provided some great singers w[ith] effective roles. Patti, Sembrich, and Ponselle all starred [in] the role of Elvira. A production at the Metropolitan [in] 1903 had a famous cast: Sembrich, Scotti, and Edoua[rd] de Reszke. Pauline Lucca, one of the greatest of all singe[rs,] first sang on the operatic stage in this opera, in 18[59,] when she was 18 years old.

Giovanni Martinelli as Ernani

Rosa Ponselle as Donna Elvira

country mansion of Madam Larina

Lotte Lehmann

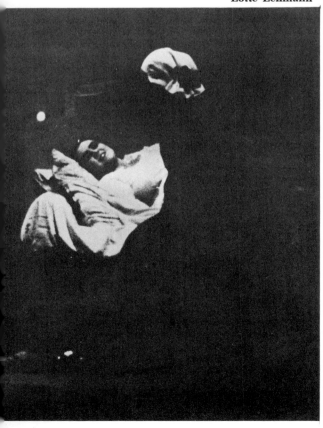

Duel between Lenski and Eugene

Eugene Onegin

Using Pushkin's tale about a pleasure loving young man and his visit to a country estate and the love affair he has there with the daughter of the family, Peter Tschaikowsky's brother Modeste created a libretto which served the composer well. *Eugene Onegin* is Tschaikowsky's most popular opera, and only it and *Pique Dame,* of the dozen he wrote, still hold the stage. It was a failure at its premiere in Moscow in 1879, but restaged at St. Petersburg five years later, it became a tremendous success and greatly increased the fame of the composer. Emilio de Gorgorza sang Onegin in a Carnegie Hall concert version under Walter Damrosch in 1908, but it was 1920 before the opera was heard in an Italian version at the Met. De Luca, Muzio, Didur, and Martinelli sang, but it was given only 7 times.

Frieda Hempel with Johannes Sembach

Johannes Sembach, Frieda Hempel and Arthur Middleton

**Margarete Ober
and Hermann Weil**

Euryanthe

Von Weber's opera *Euryanthe* has an absurd story about 12th Century France, which is basically the same tale Shakespeare told far better in his play *Cymbeline*. The opera was a failure at first, and has had no lasting success, despite occasionally brilliant revivals, such as Toscanini's at the Met in 1914, with Frieda Hempel. It reached America in 1887, at the Metropolitan, with Anton Siedl conducting a luminous cast: Lilli Lehmann, Marianne Brandt, and Max Alvary. It has been peformed only 9 times at the Metropolitan, and not once since 1915. The world premiere was in Vienna, in 1823.

Maria Jeritza as Fedora

La Favorita

Donizetti used pseudo-historical material about the favorite of Alfonso XI of Castile in fashioning his *La Favorita*. The 14th Century Spanish tale first appeared in Paris in 1840, and was soon being heard in the opera centers of the world. Leonore was one of Annie Louise Cary's roles in America. Jean de Reszke made his operatic debut in the opera, as a baritone. Five years later he sang in it again, this time the tenor role. Louise Homer first sang in opera as Leonore, and it provided Pol Plançon with a great role when it first appeared at the Metropolitan in 1895. It was heard again at the Met in the 1905 season, with Caruso and Scotti singing. Grisi and her husband Mario sang it in London, where they made it a great favorite. But like other operas with contraltos for heroines, it has languished, despite some of Donizetti's finest music.

Fedora

Sardou's lurid play about the Princess Fedora and her violent love for Count Loris, who is under suspicion of murdering her husband, provided Giordano with the subject matter for his opera *Fedora*. Caruso sang in the world premiere, and was again in the cast when the opera was produced in America at the Metropolitan in 1906, with Scotti and Lina Cavalieri. It was Cavalieri's Met debut, and she was perhaps more admired for her looks and figure than for her voice. A revival of the opera in 1923 provided Jeritza with a rich role. Martinelli and Scotti were in the cast.

Der Freischutz

Der Freischutz, the romantic tale of the freeshooter who uses the magic bullets, had a tremendous influence on the history of opera. Wagner worshipped the composer, Von Weber, and this opera is a distinct forerunner of the Wagnerian school. The romantic appeal of the opera created a sensation at the world premiere, Berlin in 1821, and Von Weber's fame was assured overnight. The part of Agathe was Jenny Lind's first role in opera, in Stockholm in 1838. The opera was given in English as early as 1825 in the United States, but has had only 17 performances at the Metropolitan.

Maria Jeritza with
Giovanni Martinelli in
"Fedora"

Lina Cavalieri made
her New York debut
as Fedora,
December 5, 1906

Enrico Caruso, Emmy Destinn and Pasquale Amato

The Girl of the Golden West

Puccini had enjoyed pleasant relations with David Belasco when dealing with him over *Madama Butterfly,* and wished to continue the relationship, using the celebrated stage director as a collaborator on his next work. His use of Belasco's play *The Girl of the Golden West* was not successful, despite a premiere at the Metropolitan which excited world-wide interest. The melodrama of the wild West had Caruso, Destinn, and Amato in the cast, Toscanini in the pit, and Puccini and Belasco hovering nearby. There were double prices, and a huge press coverage at that 1910 production, but the preposterous libretto dampened the cordial reception. It lasted only four seasons. A revival in 1929 for Jeritza, Martinelli, and Tibbett was no more successful.

Enrico Caruso as Johnson

Carolina White as Minnie

Emmy Destinn, Enrico Caruso and Pasquale Amato

Titta Ruffo as Hamlet

Emma Calvé as Ophelia

Nellie Melba as Ophelia

Hamlet

Ambroise Thomas' version of Shakespeare's *Hamlet*, by way of the frequently silly libretto provided by Barbier and Carré, has been a staple of the repertory in France ever since its world premiere at the Grand Opera in 1868, with Christine Nilsson as Ophelia and Faure in the title role. London saw it in 1869 in Italian as 'Amleto'. In 1872 Nilsson and Annie Louise Cary sang it, but it has been infrequently done here since. The principal role is a baritone, and it has met the fate of all such operas. Lasalle sang it in 1892, and Sembrich was the first Metropolitan Ophelia. Melba sang it at the Met in 1897, and Ruffo was Hamlet in Chicago in the early 1900's, and again in New York in 1920.

The Jewels of the Madonna

Wolf-Ferrari's lurid melodrama about modern day Naples
had its first production in Berlin in 1911, but it has been
in Chicago, strangely enough, that *The Jewels of the
Madonna* has enjoyed a real cult. The American premiere
took place there in 1912, with White and Sammarco singing, and Campanini conducting. It was an immediate
sensation. Rosa Raisa and her husband Giacomo Rimini
sang it often, and made their New York debuts in the
opera in 1918. The Metropolitan produced it for Jeritza
in 1925. She got 20 curtain calls after the final act, but
the opera lasted only two seasons.

The Juggler of Notre Dame

The Juggler of Notre Dame, by Jules Massenet, is a miracle play with music composed originally for male voices.
Maurice Renaud sang in it at the world premiere in
Monte Carlo in 1902. The story of the poor juggler who
performs for the statue of the Virgin Mary appealed to
Mary Garden, and she persuaded Massenet to adapt the
title role for soprano. It became a vehicle for her, and
for many years she sang it with great success. With her
retirement, *The Juggler*, Massenet's least effective score,
has vanished from the repertory.

Mary Garden as the
Juggler of Notre Dame

Carolina White
in "The Jewels of The Madonna"

The King's Henchmen

Deems Taylor's *The King's Henchman* enjoyed 14 performances in three seasons at the Metropolitan, which had commissioned the work. The 1927 premiere established Taylor as a serious composer, and with Florence Easton, Edward Johnson, and Lawrence Tibbett singing the fine literate text provided by Edna St. Vincent Millay, the production became front page news all over the country. The opera has a legendary flavor to it, though the characters are historical, and is reminiscent in mood and plot to *Pelleas* and *Tristan*. It was the first American work to be done at the Metropolitan since 1917.

**Edward Johnson with Florence Easton
in "The King's Henchman"**

**Edward Johnson
as Aethelwold**

Geraldine Farrar as The Goose Girl

Hermann Jadlowker as the King's son

Koenigskinder

Humperdinck's *Koenigskinder*, a rather wistful and sad tale about a King's daughter who is forced to act as a goose girl by an old witch who has cast a spell upon her, had its first production at the Metropolitan in 1910. Geraldine Farrar sang, supported by Louise Homer, Adamo Didur, and Pini-Corsi. The composer was present, and Alfred Hertz conducted. Until the war banished German works, *Koenigskinder* enjoyed some popularity, mostly because it provided Farrar with one of her happiest parts. At the premiere she responded to the huge ovation by taking a curtain call with a live goose in her arms. The work has seldom been done elsewhere.

Farrar and Jadlowker

Otto Goritz as the Fiddler

Madam Sans-Gene

Sardou's play *Madam Sans-Gene* not only made a successful vehicle for Farrar in Giordano's opera, it was also a great success for Ellen Terry and Sir Henry Irving. Caterina, the heroine, is a spirited French washer-woman who becomes elevated after the revolution. She rejoices in her old crude ways, much to the embarrassment of Napoleon, who finally attempts to banish her from the court. She shows him one of his old unpaid laundry bills, and he relents enough to allow her to stay on. The world premiere was at the Metropolitan in 1915. Farrar, Martinelli, Althouse, Amato, and de Segurola sang, with Toscanini conducting. In the next 4 years there were 12 repetitions, but it has been unheard since 1918.

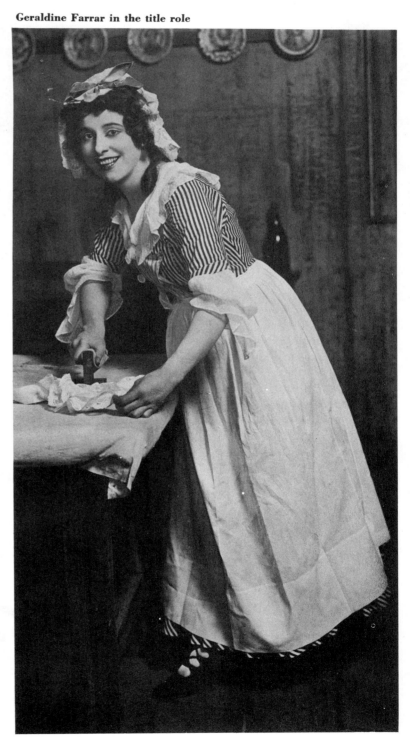

Geraldine Farrar in the title role

Giovanni Martinelli, Geraldine Farrar with Pasquale Amato

Pasquale Amato
as Napoleon

Martinelli
and Farrar

Antonio Scotti as Chim-Fen

L'Oracolo

Ponchielli's pupil Franco Leoni is known in America only as the composer of *L'Oracolo*, though he composed many other operas. Adapted from the play *The Cat and the Cherub*, *L'Oracolo* has San Francisco's Chinatown as its locale. The lurid horror tale provided Scotti with a chance to make up and act, which he did superbly. He played the role of Chim Fen 44 times at the Met, and it was the role of his final performance in 1933, ending a career spanning 34 years in New York alone. On that afternoon *L'Oracolo* followed a matinee of *Boheme*. Farrar threw a bouquet from the orchestra, and the sentimental audience heard the ageing baritone say, "I do not want to leave you, but I must". The opera was first given in London in 1905, and at the Met in 1915, with Scotti and Bori.

The Pearl Fishers

Bizet's *The Pearl Fishers* was first heard in Paris in 1863. The feeble libretto cannot completely dim the efforts of a vigorous musician, and the opera has had a sporadic career. In 1896 Calvé sang it at the Metropolitan, though only two of its three acts were performed. The rest of the program was given over to *La Navarraise*. The first Met performance was a failure and the opera was withdrawn until 1916 when it opened the season with Caruso, Hempel, De Luca, and Rothier singing. Even with such a cast and a sumptuous production, it had only three performances.

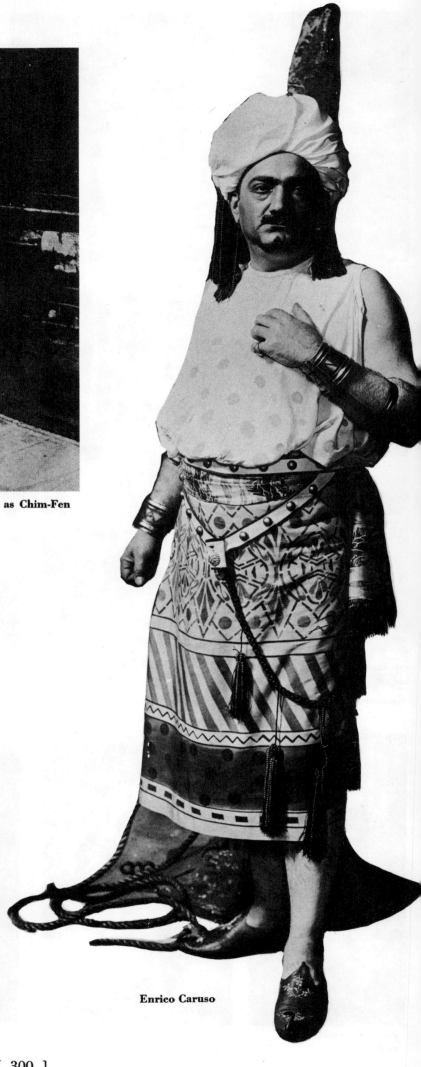

Enrico Caruso

Giuseppe De Luca, Frieda Hempel, Enrico Caruso and Leon Rothier

Hempel, Caruso and Rothier with dancing chorus

Hempel and Rothier

Ellen volunteers to bring the boy home

Brian Sullivan as Peter

Frederick Jagel as Peter

Peter convinces the drinkers that he is mad

Polyna Stoska as Ellen

Peter Grimes

Peter Grimes, by Britten, was given its world premiere at Sadler's Wells in 1945, with Peter Pears in the title role. The opera enjoyed popularity abroad and was first heard in America at the summer Berkshire Festival, where Leonard Bernstein conducted. The Metropolitan premiere took place two years later, in 1948, with Jagel as the first Grimes. Later he was succeeded by Brian Sullivan who made a great success in the role. Though the sea story generated considerable mood, the production was nondescript and the opera was not repeated after the next season.

I Puritani

I Puritani requires a tenor of phenomenal range, and several other highly gifted singers. Perhaps for that reason it is seldom performed today. This Bellini work shows many evidences of Rossini's close association with his protege. The story takes place in Plymouth during the wars between Cromwell and the Stuarts. It reached the stage in 1835, with Giulia Grisi and Rubini in the cast. Lablache, the greatest bass of his era, frequently sang in it, as did Gerster and Sembrich, who first appeared on any stage as Elvira in Athens in 1877. In 1883 she sang in the Metropolitan's first season in the role, and the opera was a vehicle for Allesandro Bonci's American debut in 1906. Tetrazzini sang Elvira, and a revival at the Met in 1917 had an all-star Spanish cast, Barrientos, Hipolito Lazaro, and José Mardones. The opera is Bellini's most mature and dramatic work.

Giuseppe De Luca as Riccardo

Maria Barrientos with Hipolito Lazaro

The Rakes Progress

Stravinsky's *The Rake's Progress*, using the Hogarth material, was widely performed in Europe after its initial premiere in Venice at the Fenice. The western hemisphere premiere was at the Metropolitan in 1953, with the composer supervising. Though it provided an interesting role for Blanche Thebom, who appeared as a bearded Turkish lady, the opera found no favor and was withdrawn after a few performances.

Blanche Thebom as the bearded Turkish lady

La Sonnambula

ne of the most popular works of the older style of Italian
pera, Bellini's *La Sonnambula* had a great vogue during
he last century, but is seldom performed today. The
remiere was in Milan in 1831, and by 1835 the opera
ad reached America, where it was frequently sung by
erster and Patti at the Academy of Music, and by Sem-
rich and Tetrazzini at the Metropolitan. It was a favorite
f Jenny Lind's, and was the first opera to be heard in
hicago, in 1850. There is a charm and sweetness about
e opera and a simple and easily understood plot, high-
ghted by a sleepwalking scene for the heroine.

**Scenes from the New York City
Opera Company production**

**Giacomo Lauri-Volpi as Calaf with
Maria Jeritza as Princess Turandot**

Turandot

urandot, Puccini's last opera, was incomplete at his
eath. Finished by Franco Alfano, it appeared at La
cala in 1926 with Raisa in the title role and Toscanini
onducting. The Metropolitan premiere took place the
ame year with Jeritza as the cruel princess, a role some
id Puccini wrote for her. Lauri-Volpi and De Luca were
lso in the cast. The next season opened with *Turandot*
nd it was given 21 times in all. A recent production at
e New York City Center was successful. The story is
rom a poetic drama by Schiller, based on an old Chinese
egend about the princess who slays those who love her.

Giuseppe Danise as William Tell

Rosa Ponselle as Mathilde

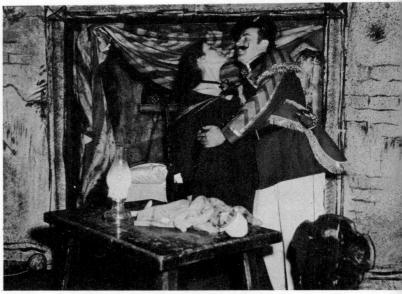

Patricia Neway and Harold Vandenberg and a scene
from the "Wozzeck" production of the New York City Opera Company

William Tell

Famous today chiefly for its overture, *William Tell* is a
grand opera on the most heroic scale. The excessive length
(six hours uncut) makes production difficult, but it contains much of Rossini's finest music. The story of the 13th
Century Swiss patriot provides a fine role for a baritone,
and Tamagno and Edouard de Reszke made the most of
the opportunities. The opera was first performed in Paris
in 1829. The Metropolitan premiere took place in·1884,
with Marianne Brandt singing a small role.

Wozzeck

Alban Berg's 1922 opera *Wozzeck* is the only modern opera
to hold its own in the German repertory, despite advanced
theories of musical composition and a story of the most
morbid psycho-sexuality. Wozzeck is a poor servant whose
association with the whore Marie leads to her murder.
The extremely difficult music required 137 rehearsals before the Berlin premiere, but caused a furore when it was
first heard. A Philadelphia concert version in 1931,
Stokowski conducting, was repeated in New York the
same year to great acclaim, yet the opera has not yet been
produced at the Metropolitan, though it was given at the
New York City Center in 1952.

Geraldine Farrar

Geraldine Farrar with Giulio Crimi

Geraldine Farrar as Zaza

Kathleen Howard with Geraldine Farrar

Zaza

Thousands of people saw Mrs. Leslie Carter play *Zaza*, and many more heard Farrar in the role after Leoncavallo made an opera of it. Produced in Milan in 1900, the opera was seen in San Francisco in 1903 at the Tivoli Opera House, but it was not until Farrar made an unexpected success of it at the Metropolitan in 1920 that it became a vogue. Belasco is given credit for the stage direction of that production, and Farrar was a sensation in a role perfectly suited to her gaiety and recklessness. She sang it 20 times in her three remaining seasons with that company, and it was the opera of her farewell, at a 1922 matinee. It has not been heard since. At her farewell, the 'Gerry-Flappers' hung banners from the boxes, sailed balloons in the air, and created a traffic jam in the streets around the opera house when the diva drove off for the last time.

Rosemary Kuhlmann, Chet Allen, and William Starling in *Amahl and the Night Visitors*

Rosemary Kuhlmann, Michael Pollock, Lawrence Winters, Richard Wentworth in *Amahl and the Night Visitors*

Menotti Operas

The Italian-born American composer, Gian-Carlo Menotti' delightful comic opera *Amelia Goes to the Ball*, remi niscent of Wolf-Ferrari in spirit, was given its worl premiere at the Curtis Institute of Music, Philadelphia in 1937, and in New York a few days later. In 193 Muriel Dickson and John Brownlee sang it at the Metro politan where it received a total of six performances in two seasons. Menotti's other works, *The Medium*, *The Consul*, both realistic operas of the verismo school, en joyed profitable Broadway runs and are frequently per formed in Europe. His Christmas opera, *Amahl and the Night Visitors*, has been an annual event on T.V. net works for which it was commissioned.

Marie Powers, Leon Lishner, Patricia Neway in *The Consul*

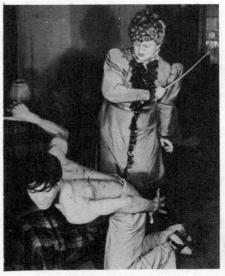

Leo Coleman and Marie Powers in *The Medium*

Opera Houses in America

The Federal Street Theatre, Boston,
opened February 3, 1794. Here
Charles Powell's company began
a series of opera performances for
several seasons.

Theatre d'Orleans, New Orleans,
where in 1813 the operas of Rossini,
Meyerbeer, Auber and Donizetti
were sung in French by
Parisian singers

The New Chestnut Street Theatre, Philadelphia,
where opera was sung in 1825

Park Street Theatre, New York, where Garcia presented nine Italian operas in 1825

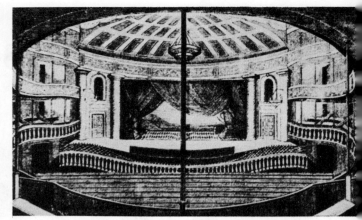

Interior of the Park Street Theatre, 1825

The Italian Opera House, New York, the first building in America erected exclusively for opera, opened November 18, 1833, with Rossini's "La Gazza Ladra"

Palmos Opera House on Chambers Street, New York, opened February 3, 1844, with Bellini's "I Puritani"

Interior of Palmos Opera House (1844)

Interior of Castle Garden where Jenny Lind first appeared in concert, September 11, 1850

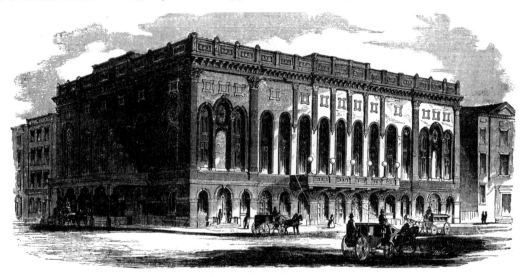

The Academy of Music opened its doors at Fourteenth Street and Irving Place, New York, in 1854

The Second Jenny Lind Theatre, San Francisco. As early as 1854 there were eleven opera houses in this town

The Academy of Music, Philadelphia, was built in 1857 and is still in use today

Niblo's Gardens, New York, where Wagner's operas were first sung in America in 1859

Interior of Niblo's Theatre (1855)

Crosby Opera House, Chicago, built in 1865

The Manhattan Opera House on
Thirty-Fourth Street

The Boston Opera House

The St. Louis Municipal Auditorium

The Metropolitan Opera House, New York, 1884

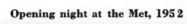
Opening night at the Met, 1952

Exterior of Metropolitan Opera House, 1953

The Met proscenium and orchestra pit

Interior shot of the Met

Opening of the Auditorium Theatre, Chicago, December 10, 1889. First performance was "Romeo and Juliet" with Adelina Patti and Perugini singing the title roles and Sapio, conducting

War Memorial Opera House, San Francisco

The Civic Opera House, Chicago, opened on November 4, 1929 with a performance of "Aida" with the following cast: Rosa Raisa, Charles Marshall, Cesare Formichi, Cyrena Van Gordon, Virgilio Lazzari, and Chase Baromeo, and Giorgic Polacco, conducting.

Index